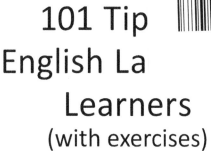

101 Tip
English La
Learners
(with exercises)

Michael McCarthy

Cover by tebbitdesign

http://tebbitdesign.co.uk/

Prolinguam Publishing 2019

Prolinguam Publishing
7 CB23 2RW
UK

Copyright © Michael McCarthy 2019

All rights reserved

Minor changes have been made to the wording of this edition compared with that of the e-book edition of 2019 for formatting reason

Dedicated to the memory of my late friend and colleague
Professor Ronald Carter

About this book

This book contains 101 tips for learners of English (at high B1, and B2 and above CEFR levels) who are interested in what is considered correct in standard British English. Much of it also applies to the standard English of other parts of the world where English is a first or dominant language. The tips come from the author's notebooks and observations recorded during more than 50 years of involvement in the teaching of English. Many of the tips are about common problems that learners encounter and things which most native speakers and expert users would consider to be errors of grammar, vocabulary or spelling. Other tips are just general advice on using English in different situations. There special tips for students of academic English, and there are exercises at the end of the book.

And why 101 tips? Well, if you write 100 tips, there's always another one …

How to use the book

You can look up words in the contents or go to the appropriate letter of the alphabet or read the book from start to finish. Each entry gives at least one example sentence. The examples are all correct usage. If there are typical mistakes which learners make, the incorrect forms are written with strikethrough (e.g. ~~She's engineer~~). Not all the errors may be relevant to you. It depends on your first language. However, they are typical errors which the author has collected over many years of teaching, reading learners' essays and listening to their spoken English. You can test yourself with the exercises at the end of the book.

CONTENTS

A

1 A/an

A common problem is using *one* instead of *a/an*.
One is a number, meaning 'not two or more'.
A/an is the indefinite article. It is used to refer
to someone or something as a member of a
type or class of people or things.
*I went to Berlin to visit **a** friend.* (~~one friend~~)
I have just one friend living in London. (not two,
not or three, etc.)
We use *a/an* to talk about people's jobs.
*She is **an** engineer.* (~~She's engineer~~)
We don't use *a/an* before uncountable nouns.
I've got some good news for you. (~~a good news~~)
See Countable nouns
See Uncountable nouns

According to
See Opinion, view, point of view

Above
See Prepositions

Accommodation
See Uncountable nouns

2 Abroad

Abroad is an adverb, so we do not use *to* before
it. It means 'to or in another/a foreign country'.
*I'd like to go **abroad** and work for a while in a
different culture.* (~~go to abroad~~)
*It was exciting, as it was my first trip **abroad**.*
(~~my first trip to abroad~~)

3   Across, over and through

Across, over and *through* are prepositions or adverbs.

Across

Across is used to refer to going from one side to another of something (e.g. a road, a river, a bridge).

*We swam **across** the river and rested on the bank on the other side.* (preposition)

*We don't need a boat. The river is only about 20 metres wide; we can swim **across**.* (adverb)

Across can also be used to refer to location.

*As you come out of the hotel, there's a Japanese restaurant just **across** the road.* (i.e. on the other side of the road)

Over

Over is similar to *across but* is often used to refer to movement which goes up then down.

*We climbed **over** the fence and walked **across** the field.*

*They built a new bridge **over** the river to ease the traffic congestion on the old one.*

Through

Through is used for movement from one side to the other of something when it is all around you.

*We walked **through** the forest until we came to an old ruined building.*

*The train goes **through** several tunnels before it reaches the top of the mountain.*

*The doctor is ready to see you. Would you like to come **through**?* (i.e. through the building to the doctor's office)

4   Actual and actually

Actual and *actually* are used to talk about things which are real or true or surprising. They are not used to refer to the present time.
*Everyone calls him Charlie, but his **actual** name is Robert. Charlie is just his middle name.*
A: *His name is Carlos. Is he Spanish?* B: *No, he's from Cuba **actually**.*
*She **actually** told the teacher he was the worst teacher she had ever had!* (surprising fact)
To talk about time, we can use expressions such as *at the moment, at present* or *right now*.
***Right now,** I'm sharing a flat, but I'd like to buy one of my own.* (~~Actually, I'm ...~~)

5   Address

Note the spelling: two *d*'s:
*Do you know Miguel's **add**ress?* (~~adress~~)

6   Adjectives with -ing and -ed

Some adjectives have two forms, one ending in *-ing* and one ending in *-ed*, for example *interesting/interested, boring/bored, amazing/amazed, surprising/surprised*.
The *-ing* forms are for a person or thing that *causes* something, the *-ed* forms are for the person who experiences it.
*It was an **interesting** lecture, but I got a bit **bored** towards the end.* (~~I got a bit boring~~)
*I was **amazed** to hear that the flight only cost 300 dollars. I thought it would be much more.* (~~I was amazing~~)

7 Adverbs

Most adverbs end in -*ly*. Be careful not to use the adjective form without -*ly* when describing an action.

*She sang so **beautifully**.* (~~so beautiful~~)
*The essay was very **badly** written.* (~~bad written~~)

Don't put adverbs between a verb and its object.

*I don't speak Russian **very well**.* (~~I don't speak very well Russian~~)
*I'm giving up my job **next month**.* (~~I'm giving up next month my job~~).

In more formal contexts, if the object is a very long phrase (underlined in the example), an adverb can sometimes be used between the verb and object.

*She will give up **next month** <u>a job she has devoted her whole life to</u>.*

See Always

Advice
See Uncountable nouns

Against
See Prepositions

8 Afford

Afford is used with *can, could* or forms of *be able*. Be careful with the spelling. Students often write *efford* or *effort* instead of *afford*.

*I cycle everywhere. I can't **afford** a car.*
*She'd like **to be able to afford** to go on holiday, but she has to pay her college fees.*

We normally use *afford* with a *to*-infinitive,

though you will sometimes see it used with an
-*ing* form.
I ***can't afford to buy*** *new clothes. I'll just have
to wear my old ones.*

9 Ago

Don't confuse *ago* and *before*. We use *ago* to
look back to a point in time in relation to now.
Before can be used to look back to a point in
time earlier than another time in the past.
*I lived in Berlin ten years **ago**.* (~~ten years before~~)
*I got to know Luisa at the conference last year. I
had met her for the first time a couple of years
before that.*
Don't use *for* with *ago*.
*She moved to Australia three years **ago**.* (~~for
three years ago~~)

10 Already

We use *already* to refer to things which happen
before something else, often unexpectedly.
*When we got there, the train had **already** left.*
Note the spelling: just one *l*: *already* (~~allready~~).
In British English, we normally use the present
perfect or past perfect with *already*.
*Have you **already** eaten?* (~~Did you already eat?~~)
*She'd **already** left when I arrived.* (~~She already
left~~)
In other varieties of English, you may hear the
past tense used with *already*.

Also
See Even

11 Although, though, even though

Although and *though* are often both correct. *Although* is slightly more formal. They are used to express a contrast.

Although/Though *the water was cold, we really enjoyed our swim in the river.*

Although always comes at the beginning of the clause. *Though* can come in the middle or at the end of the clause when it means 'but' or 'however'.

It's good that the flight isn't until midday. We should leave early, **though***. We don't know how long it will take to get to the airport.* (~~although~~)

Even though is used to make a stronger, or unexpected, contrast.

I feel as if we've always been friends, **even though** *I only met him for the first time a month ago.*

12 Always

We don't normally start sentences with *always*. It usually goes between the subject and the verb.

I **always** *say hello to my neighbour, but she never says hello to me.* (~~Always I say hello~~)

We can start a sentence with *always* when it is a command or an instruction.

Always *use a different password for each different website.*

13 Amount of and number of

A*mount of* is used with uncountable nouns (e.g.

food, furniture, information, money, equipment).
*That's a huge **amount of food** for two people.*
*He spent a great **amount of time** revising his essay because he wanted it to be perfect.*
Number of is used for nouns in the plural.
*I have met the President **a number of times** as he is a friend of my father's.*
***The number of road accidents** has fallen over the last five years.*
However, you will often see and hear people using *amount of* with plural nouns.
***The amount of problems** young people have nowadays is very different from when I was young.*
Subject-verb agreement with *number of* depends on whether we say *a number of* or *the number of*. *A number of* takes a plural verb:
***A number of cases** of thefts from parked cars **have** been reported in the local newspaper recently.*
The number of takes a singular verb:
***The number of thefts** from parked cars **has** increased recently.*
A number of is normally used with *there are*, even though *a number* is singular:
***There are a number of things** we need to decide.*

14 As

In academic writing, we often use *as* with a past participle or with a passive voice verb, but without using *it*. This is common when referring to tables and figures or to other people's work/ research.
*The population increased sharply after 1980, **as***

shown in table 2. (~~as it is shown~~)
As can be seen in the annual report, the company made a small profit in 2016.
We can use *as* and invert the subject and an auxiliary verb when two people or things do the same action.
Her father worked in a factory, **as did** *my father.* (both fathers did the same thing)
See Inversion
See Passive voice

15   As and like

Don't use *as* on its own to introduce an example or examples of something. Use *like*.
We could eat something light around midday, **like** *a sandwich or a salad, then have dinner later.* (~~as a sandwich or a salad~~)
Such as can be used to introduce examples.
Languages which are quite different from English, **such as** *Chinese or Korean, can be difficult for English speakers to learn.* (~~as Chinese or Korean~~)
As and *like* followed by nouns have two different meanings.
As *your father, I want you to do your best.* (I *am* your father)
Like *your father, I want you to do your best.*
(I am *not* your father, but I share his feelings/ views)

16   As well

Don't start a sentence with *as well* on its own.
Use *also*, or in more formal academic contexts,

use *in addition*.

*We need three tables for the meeting. **Also**, we need 20 chairs.* (As well we need)

*The team collected data from medical records. **In addition**, they carried out interviews with patients.*

As well normally goes at the end of the sentence, and is similar to using *too*. It is less formal than *also* or *in addition*.

*Freda was at the party and George was there **as well**.* (or: George was there too)

We can start a sentence with *as well as* to introduce the first item in a list.

***As well as** working at a school on weekdays, he has a part-time job in the evenings and coaches a swimming team at weekends.*

See Too

At

See Prepositions

17 At last, lastly, finally

We use *at last* to talk about things which we have waited for, or which have taken longer than we wanted or expected.

*This is the third time I've taken my driving test and I've passed it **at last**!*

We do not use *at last* for the final item in a list or at the end of something. We use *lastly* or *finally*.

(at the end of a speech) ***Lastly/Finally**, I would like to thank you all for coming to the meeting today.* (At last, I would like ...)

B

18 Because

In writing, don't start a new sentence with *because* when it completes the meaning of the previous sentence.

*I'm going to train to be a primary school teacher **because** I have always wanted to work with young children.* (... a primary school ~~teacher. Because~~ I have always wanted ...)

You can start a new sentence with *because* when it looks forward to the rest of the sentence.

***Because** I have always wanted to work with young children, I'm going to train to be a primary school teacher.*

19 Before

Before comes after a time expression when it refers to a time in the past. It acts like the past tense of *ago*.

*I worked with Carmen last year in the children's camp. We had met **two years before**, at another kids' camp.* (~~before two years~~)

Before is followed by the *-ing* form of a verb, not the *to*-infinitive.

***Before leaving** the office, he left a note on Clara's desk.* (~~Before to leave~~)

See Ago

20 Below

When we use *below* to refer to something that comes later in a text, it follows the noun.
The statistics are interesting. See the table below. (~~the below table~~)

21 Born

We normally use the past tense with *born.*
I was born in 1998. (~~I am born~~)

22 Borrow

Don't confuse *borrow* and *lend.* If you borrow something, you receive it and you keep it for a time.
*I missed the bus, so I **borrowed** my brother's bike to go to school that day.* (~~lent my brother's bike~~)
See Lend

23 Bring and take

If someone *brings* something or someone to a place, they move it from somewhere else to where the speaker is, was or will be.
*When you come to my house on Thursday, **bring** your guitar.* (the speaker will be at home on Thursday)
If someone *takes* something or someone to a place, they move it from where the speaker is, was or will be, to somewhere else.
*Are you going out? **Take** an umbrella. I think it's going to rain.* (the umbrella will go from 'here'

to another place).

By

See Passive voice

See Prepositions

 C

24 Can and could

Can refers to abilities and things which are facts.

*She **can** run a marathon in under five hours.* (she is able to, and has done it)

*It **can** rain a lot in Ireland in October.* (we know this because it is true)

Could is used when something is possible, but we do not know if it is true.

*Take an umbrella. It **could** rain later.* (rain is possible, but we do not know for certain)

Could is also used as a past-tense form of *can*.

*When I was younger, I **could** run much faster.*

We also use *can* to ask permission. It is less formal than *may* or *could*.

***Can** I leave before the end of class today, please?*

Students often overuse *could*, especially after *I hope*.

*I hope we **can** meet soon to discuss our plans.* (I~~ hope we could meet~~)

*In the park there is an area where little children **can** play safely.* (~~could play~~)

If this sentence was past tense, then *could* would be correct.

*In the park there **was** an area where little children **could** play safely.*

25 Commas

Commas and lists

We use commas to separate the items in a list, except before *and* when it introduces the final item in the list.

*There were three chairs**,** a bookshelf**,** a table **and** a sofa in the room.*

However, American English often prefers a comma before *and* in these cases.

Commas and subordinate clauses

When a subordinate clause (e.g. a clause starting with *if, when, because, before, after*) comes before the main clause, we use a comma.

*If you would like to stay with us for a couple of days**,** please let me know.*

When the subordinate clause comes after the main clause, we do not need a comma.

I'll cook dinner for us when you get home from work.

See Relative clauses

Commas after sentence connectors

We often use commas with sentence connectors.

He made a loss three years in a row.
***Consequently,** he had to sell his business.*

*You are not allowed to park at the school gates. You may**, however,** drop your children off there when bringing them to school.*

See However
See Because

No comma between subject and verb

Don't use a comma between the subject and the verb, even if the subject is quite long

(underlined here).
The one thing about buying online that always
annoys me is *when a website wants too many*
personal details from you. (The one thing about
buying online that always annoys ~~me, is~~ when ...)

26 Comparative

Use *than* after a comparative, not *that*.
The new phone is more expensive **than** *the old*
model. (~~more expensive that~~)
When we compare two people or things, we use
a comparative, not a superlative.
She has two brothers. The **older** *brother lives*
in London and the **younger** *brother lives in*
Manchester. (~~oldest~~ / ~~youngest~~)
That of can be used in comparisons instead of
repeating a noun. This is common in academic
writing.
Her salary is greater than **that of** *a university*
professor. (i.e. greater than the salary of ...)
This can be expressed less formally by using a
possessive 's:
*Her salary is greater than a university lecturer***'s***.*
That of is used after expressions such as *the*
same as, similar to, equivalent to, different
from/to, greater/less than, like and comparable
to/with.
See More
See Superlatives

27 Concentrate

Don't use a reflexive pronoun (*myself, yourself,*
etc.) with the verb *concentrate*. It does not need
any object.

*I'm not good at studying for exams. I find it difficult to **concentrate**.* (~~concentrate myself~~)
If we want to use an object, we use *concentrate on*.
*You should stop playing computer games and **concentrate on** studying for your exam!*

Conditional
See If

28 Consider and regard

We normally use *to be*, not *as*, with *consider*.
*Many people **consider** Rome **to be** Europe's most beautiful city.* (~~consider Rome as~~)
Use *as* with *regard*.
*She is **regarded as** one of the best novelists of the present decade.*

Could
See Can and could

29 Countable nouns

A countable noun (e.g. *book, car, child, computer, flower*) almost always needs a determiner (e.g. *a, the, my, this*) in front of it when it is singular.
*He gave me **a** lovely **present** for my birthday.* (~~gave me lovely present~~)
*She spends hours on **her computer**.* (~~on computer~~)
When a countable noun is plural, it can be used without a determiner if it refers to a whole class of people or things.
***Trains** are much better for the environment than **cars** and **lorries**.*
See Uncountable nouns

Depend
See Prepositions

30 Do and make

Students often confuse *do* and *make*. *Do* focuses on activities and actions. *Make* focuses on the product or result of activities and actions.

Activities: *do your homework, do the shopping, do some work, do an exam, do an experiment, do research, do business*

We **did** some **sightseeing** in the old town.

Products/results of activities: *make dinner, make a mistake, make a decision, make progress, make a noise, make a note of something, make a phone call*

We're going to **make a video** about our school.

The best advice is to memorise the combinations, as in the lists above, and always make a note of any new combinations you encounter (e.g. *make a payment, do a marathon, make an effort, do your best*)

Don't use *make* with *photograph(s)*. Use *take*. We **took** a lot of photographs in the old town. (~~made~~)

Emphasise
See Prepositions

Equipment
See Uncountable nouns

31 Especially and specially

Especially means 'particularly' or 'above all'.
*I love her novels, **especially** her first one.*
Specially is used to refer to a specific or unique purpose of something.
*The company makes office chairs **specially** designed for those who spend hours at a computer.*
In informal speaking, *especially* often sounds like *specially*. The difference is more important in writing.

32 Even

Don't confuse *even* and *also*. We use *also* to add something.
*Cycling is good for the environment. It is **also** good for your health.* (~~It is even good for your health~~)
Even is used when something is unexpected or surprising.
*She's an amazing musician: she can **even** sing and play the violin at the same time!*
See Although, though, even though

33 Ever

Use *ever*, not *never*, after a negative verb.
*I promise you I won't **ever** be late again.*
(~~I won't never be late~~)
Ever since is written as two words.
*I've always left a key with my neighbour **ever**

since I locked myself out of my flat. (~~eversince~~)

34 Every

Don't use *every* with uncountable nouns.
All *the furniture was new.* (~~Every furniture~~)
As two words, *every day* is an adverb or noun phrase.
*He phones his parents **every day**.* (adverb phrase)
Every day *brings more terrible news about the war.* (noun phrase)
Everyday written as one word is an adjective.
Everyday *English is quite different from formal, academic English.*

35 Everyone

Everyone is followed by a singular verb.
*Everyone **was** happy when they heard the good news.* (~~Everyone were happy~~)
It can be written as two words (with *of*) when it means 'all' or 'every single one'.
Every one *of the tickets was sold within minutes of them going on sale online.*
See Pronouns ending in *-body* and *-one*

36 Expect, hope, wait for, wish

Students often confuse these verbs.

Expect
If you *expect* something, you are saying you think or are sure it will happen.
*I have to stay at home this morning. **I'm expecting** a parcel with some things I ordered online.*

Hope

If you *hope* that something is true or will happen, you do not know if it is true, but you want it to be.

*I **hope** it's fine tomorrow. We're going on a hike.*
*I **hope** you had a good holiday last week.*

Wait for

If you *wait for* something, you let the time pass until it happens or arrives.

*We stood at the station and **waited for** the bus for over an hour, but it never arrived.*

Wish

If you *wish* something, you want the situation to be different or better than now. We use *wish* with a past-tense verb or a past modal verb (*would, could, should*).

*I **wish** I **had** a bigger apartment.*
*I **wish** you **would** stop making a noise. I'm trying to study.*
*I **wish** I **could** play the cello. I love the sound of it.*

We use *wish* for special occasions and important events when we want them to be pleasant.

*She **wished** me a happy birthday.*
*I **wish** you good luck in your exams.*

F

37 Far

Use *far* in questions and negative sentences.
*How **far** is it to the nearest railway station?*
*Is the stadium **far** from here?*

*The hotel was **not far** from the main square, so it was in a good location for sightseeing.*
You can use *a long way* in affirmative sentences.
*The museum is **a long way** from here, so we'll have to get a bus or a taxi.*

38 Few and a few

Few has a slightly negative meaning ('not many / not as many as needed, hoped for or expected').
***Few** people have ever experienced space travel.*
A few means 'a small number' but with a positive meaning.
*We have **a few** minutes before the train leaves. Shall we get some coffee?*

39 Figures and tables

In academic English, when we refer to a figure or a table which is numbered, we do not use *the*.
***Table 2** shows that there was a rise in the population between 1990 and 2000. (~~The table 2~~)*
*The city is divided into three major zones (see **figure 1**, below). (~~the figure 1~~)*
We can use *the* if we do not mention a number.
***The table** you see on the screen shows the economic statistics for 2010.*

40 Find

Find is the present tense and infinitive form.
Found is the past form.
*I need to **find** a flat to rent for the autumn. (~~I~~*

~~need to found~~)
When *find* is followed by an adjective (e.g. *difficult, easy, amazing*), we use *it* after the verb.
*I find **it** difficult to pronounce Swedish surnames.* (~~I find difficult~~)

41 First, at first, firstly

We use *at first* when something in a situation has changed.
***At first**, I was homesick when I went to live abroad, but after a month or so, I got used to it and felt more at home.*
We use *first* and (more formally) *firstly* to introduce a list of things.
***First**, I would like to thank you all for coming here today. Next, I would like to welcome our new members.* (~~At first, I would like~~)

For
See Prepositions

42 Fun

When *fun* is used as a noun, don't use *very*.
*The party was **great fun**.* (~~The party was very fun~~)
Fun can be used as an adjective.
*They often organise **fun** events for children.*
Don't confuse *fun* with *funny*. *Funny* means that someone/something makes you laugh, or that someone/something is strange.

Furniture
See Uncountable nouns

43 Gender

Until recently, the names of a lot of jobs were gender-marked with suffixes. Most people now consider such usage as old-fashioned, inappropriate or sexist. In some cases, what used to be the male ending is used for both sexes; in others, new forms are used. Here are some examples. It is generally considered good practice to use a neutral term.

male	female	neutral
headmaster	headmistress	headteacher
policeman	policewoman	police officer
waiter	waitress	waiter, server
spokesman	spokeswoman	spokesperson
fireman	firewoman	firefighter
chairman	chairwoman	chair, chair person
manager	manageress	manager

44 Get

Don't use *get* when you talk about someone giving birth to a baby. Use *have*.

*My sister **had** a baby last week.* (~~got a baby~~)

You can use *get* with the past participle of a verb to form the passive voice. It is less formal than the passive with *be* and is often used about negative events.

*My bike **got stolen** yesterday.* (more formal: *was stolen*)

*She **got fined** £100 for parking in a prohibited area.*
See Passive voice

45 Good

Good is an adjective. *Well* is the adverb form.
*Their boss did not treat them very **well**.* (~~treat them very good~~)
In informal conversation, people often answer *'(I'm) good!'* when someone asks, *'How are you?'*. More formally, people say, *'(I'm) very well.'*

46 Home

When *home* is used after a verb, don't use *to*.
*We got **home** at midnight.* (~~to home~~)
*She came **home** early.*

Homework
See Uncountable nouns

Hope
See Expect, hope, wait for wish

47 However

In writing, we use *however* at the beginning of a sentence or at the end, or between the subject and verb and separated by a comma or commas.

*It's a wonderful country to visit. **However,** it can be difficult to find good accommodation in the smaller towns.*
*It's a wonderful country to visit. It can**, however,** be difficult to find good accommodation in the smaller towns.* (more formal, written style)
*Streaming video is easy nowadays. There can be problems with slow download speeds**, however.***
We do not normally use *however* after a comma to start a new clause. We can use a semi-colon or start a new sentence.
*The new hotel is very convenient for getting around the city centre; **however**, it is expensive.* (~~city centre, however it is~~ ...)

48 If

We don't normally use *will* and *would* in the *if-*clause in a conditional sentence. *Will* and *would* come in the main clause.
***If** she **passes** all her exams, she **will** go to university in October.* (~~If she will pass~~)
***If** I **had** a car, I **would** be able to visit my family more often.* (~~If I would have~~)
We use *had* + past participle in the *if-*clause and *would have* + past participle in the main clause to refer to possibilities in the past.
***If** I **had known** how difficult it was to get there by bus, I **would have got** a taxi.* (~~If I would have known~~)

49 If and when

We don't use *when* to talk about possibilities.
If she wins the race, she will get a place in the national team. (Not ~~When she wins~~ – we do not know that she will win)
When is used to refer to things that do happen or that we can be sure will happen.
***When** my plane lands, I'll text you.*
(I am sure my plane will land)

In and into
See Prepositions

50 Increase and decrease

When we use verbs of increase and decrease (e.g. *increase, rise, fall, decrease, drop*), we use *by* before a number.
*House prices have fallen **by** 5% this year.*
*The temperature was increased **by** 10 degrees in the second experiment.*
When we use the same words as nouns, we use *of* before a number and *in* before the thing we are referring to.
*There was an increase **of** around 100,000 **in** the population during the decade 1990-2000.*
*A drop **of** 30% **in** the price of oil in just one week caused an economic crisis.*

Infinitive
See Prepositions: For + -ing

Information
See Uncountable nouns

In front of and opposite
See Prepositions

51 Inversion

If we begin a sentence with a negative adverb such as *rarely, seldom, not only, hardly*, we invert the subject and auxiliary verb, just as we do in a question.

*Not only **did I** lose my keys, I lost my phone too.*
*Hardly **had he** arrived home from work, when someone rang the doorbell.*

If the verb is the main verb *be*, we just invert the subject and verb.

*Not only **is he** a pianist, he's a pretty good violinist too.*

After *as*, in short clauses with the substitute *do*, we invert the subject and auxiliary verb, or the subject and verb *be*.

*I congratulated her on her promotion, **as did everyone** in our team.*
*She was a secondary school teacher, **as was** her sister.*
See As

52 It's and its

It's means *'it is'*. *Its* means 'belonging to a thing or an animal'.

***It's** a good restaurant.* (= It is a good restaurant.)
*We came to a beautiful beach. **Its** sand was almost pure white.* (~~It's sand~~)
We can also use *its* to refer to something which

belongs to an animal.
*This cat has hurt **its** paw.*

Job and work
See Uncountable nouns

Journey and travel
See Uncountable nouns

Knowledge
See Uncountable nouns

53 Lend

If you *lend* something, you give it to someone to keep for a time. The past tense is *lent*.
*I **lent** him that book a year ago and he still hasn't given it back.* (~~lend / lended~~)
The word *loan* is normally used as a noun, but it is sometimes used as a verb when talking about money, especially large sums.
*He got a **loan** from the bank to start a small business.*
*Her parents **loaned** her the money to buy a car.*
See Borrow

54 Less and fewer

We use *less* with uncountable nouns, for example, *petrol, food, fun, information, money,*

work, time.
*Now that I am only working part-time, I've **got less money** to spend.*
Fewer is used with plural countable nouns, for example, *cars, books, people, problems.*
*There are **fewer buses** after six o'clock in the evening.*
You will often hear people saying *less buses, less problems, less trees*, etc. However, you should be careful not to use *less* with plural nouns in exams and very formal situations.

55 Like, love, hate and enjoy,

When we use *like, love* or *hate* with an *-ing* form, we are stressing the activity itself.
*I love **swimming** in the sea at night when the moon is shining on the water. It's magic.*
When we use *like, love* or *hate* with an infinitive, we are stressing a preference for something.
*We like **to stop** work and have coffee at about 10.30 every day.*
*I hate **to disturb** you when you're working, but I need your help in the kitchen.*
American English speakers generally use the infinitive form with these verbs more than British English speakers do.
Enjoy is always followed by an *-ing* form, not the infinitive.
*I enjoy **watching** football on TV, even though I never play football myself.*

56 Likely

British English speakers traditionally use *likely* as an adjective (followed by a *to*-infinitive), but now more and more they use *likely* as an adverb. This is probably due to the influence of North American English.

*The decision **is likely to** be taken very soon.* (adjective)

*The decision **will likely** be taken very soon.* (adverb)

57 Little and few

Little is used with uncountable nouns, for example, *petrol, fun, information, money, work, time.*

*We get very **little** information about management decisions at my workplace.*

Few is used with plural countable nouns, for example, *cars, books, people, problems.*

***Few** people realise how much information social media sites gather about them.*

See Few and a few

See Less and fewer

58 Lot and Lots

Lots of is more informal than *a lot of.*

*He's got **lots of** friends in London.* (informal)

*There are **a lot of** people who disagree with the plan.* (less informal/neutral)

See Much, many, a lot

Make
See Do and make

59 Mind (Do you / Would you?)

Do you mind and *would you mind* are both polite ways of making a request (i.e. when you want something from someone or you want them to do something).
Do you mind is most often followed by *if.*
A: **Do you mind if** *I sit next to you?*
B: **No**, *please, have this chair.*
The polite answer is *no*, because the speaker is saying 'no, I don't mind or have a problem with what you want to do'.
Would you mind can also be used in the same situation, often with a past tense.
Would you mind if *I* **sat** *next to you at dinner tonight? I don't want to sit with someone boring.*
However, *would you mind* is most often followed by an *-ing* form, and we use it to ask someone to do something.
Would you mind turning *your music down? I'm trying to write my essay and I'm finding it difficult to concentrate.*

60 More

Don't use *more* with short adjectives like *big, tall, old*, etc. in comparisons.
My brother is **taller** *than me.* (~~more tall~~)
Use *more* with longer adjectives.
Today's lecture was **more interesting** *than last week's.*
See Comparative

61 Much, many, a lot

One common problem is overuse of *much* and *many.* In the affirmative, *much* and *many* sound very formal. In most cases, *a lot of* sounds more natural.

*We have **much** work to do tomorrow.* (very formal)

*We have **a lot of work** to do tomorrow.* (more typical, more natural)

*We have **many** things to do tomorrow.* (very formal)

*We have **a lot of things** to do tomorrow.* (more typical, more natural)

Questions with *much* and *many* are open-ended. The speaker does not know if the answer will be a large or small quantity or number.

*Do you have **much** work to do for your exams?* (I have no idea if it is much or little)

*Do you have **many** cousins?* (I have no idea if the answer will be a large or small number)

Questions with *a lot of* suggest that the speaker thinks there may be a large quantity of something.

*Do you have **a lot of** work to do for your exams?* (people usually do have to work hard before exams)

*Do you have **a lot of** cousins?* (things you have said suggest that maybe you have a big family)

62 Must

Use *must* to talk about things which you feel are important obligations for yourself or others.

*I **must** get my hair cut. It's got too long.*

When the obligation comes from outside, you can use *have to, should, ought to* or *need to*, depending on how strong the obligation is.

I **have to** *register for the exam by next Monday.* (strong, external obligation)

I **should / ought to** *call my mother. I haven't been in touch with her for a couple of weeks.* (less strong)

American English often uses *need to* where British English uses *must* or *have to.*

It's six o'clock. You **need to** *leave right now, or you'll be late!*

You can also use *must* to make a guess or an assumption about someone or something.

Clare and John's car is not in their driveway. They **must** *be away.*

Using *must* in this way is very common in short responses.

A: *It's been a long journey!*

B: *Yes, you* **must** *be very tired.*

The past form of *must* for guesses and assumptions is *must have* (+ past participle).

There **must have been** *200 people at the meeting last night. It was amazing.*

N

Near and nearby
See Prepositions

63 No and none of

No can be used before a singular, plural or uncountable noun when it has no article or other determiner (e.g. *my, your, this, those*).

No teacher *is perfect, but she was certainly the best teacher I've ever had.* (singular)
No vehicles *are allowed on the hiking trails.* (plural)
No furniture *should be removed from this room.* (uncountable)
When the noun has another determiner, we must use *none of*.
None of the *furniture in the apartment belongs to me.*
None of their relatives *live near them.*
In very formal writing, *none of* takes a singular verb.
None of the stolen bicycles was *insured.* (or *were insured* in less formal situations)
Don't say *nobody of*.
None of the people *at the meeting agreed with the decision.* (~~Nobody of the people~~)

64 No and not any

No before a noun is stronger and more emphatic than *not any*.
*He doesn't have **any** friends who are the same age. All his friends seem to be much older.*
*He has **no** friends who are the same age. All his friends seem to be much older.* (stronger)

65 Not only ... (but) also

We use *not only ... (but) also* to talk about two things when the second thing adds something important or surprising to the first one.

*He's **not only** a swimming coach but **also** a member of the national team.*

If we start a sentence with *not only*, we invert the subject and verb.

*Not only **does he teach** kids to swim, he's also a champion swimmer himself.*

66 Nowadays

Nowadays is an adverb.

*People get most of their news **nowadays** from social media rather than from radio or TV.*

Don't use *nowadays* as an adjective. Use *of today,* or *present-day.*

*The youth **of today** don't appreciate how hard life was for their parents when they were young.* (~~The nowadays youth~~)

***Present-day** conditions in the refugee camps are worse than at any time in the past 20 years.*

67 Offering to do something

We normally use *will/'ll* or another modal verb such as *can* or *could* when we make an offer, not the present simple.

Your bag looks very heavy. I'll carry it for you. (~~I carry it~~)

You look very busy. I can phone Jeremy. (~~I phone~~)

On

See Prepositions

68 On the contrary, on the other hand

On the contrary is used when we want to say that the opposite of something is true.
He's not a cold person. **On the contrary**, *he's very friendly.*
On the other hand is used when we want to modify or add something important to a statement. It is often used with *on the one hand*, which comes first.
On the one hand, *she doesn't seem to see how important it is to save money for the future.* **On the other hand**, *she is very young, and she may change her attitude as she grows up.*

69 Opinion, view, point of view

We use *in my opinion* or *in my view* when we want to say what we think about something. We use *from my/his/her/etc. point of view* when we say how something affects us or someone else.
The plan cannot work, **in my opinion / in my view**. (what I think about the plan)
From my point of view, *the new tax levels are good, as I don't earn much.* (how the new tax levels affect me personally)
From a teacher's point of view, *online learning has both advantages and disadvantages.* (how online learning affects teachers)
Don't use *according to me* when you want to give an opinion. We use *according to* when we are referring to things other people have said or written.

*The concert's been cancelled, **according to** Laura.*

70 Other

Here are some guidelines for using *other*.
Other with no determiner can be used with plural nouns.

*Some cities celebrate the National Day on the nearest Saturday to April 10th; **other cities** celebrate it on the day itself.*

Another is used with singular countable nouns and with the pronoun *one*.

*There are five people coming to dinner. We need **another chair**. There's **another one** in the kitchen.*

We don't use *another* with uncountable nouns.
The most important furniture from the house will be sold next week. Other furniture will be sold at a later date. (~~Another furniture~~)

Others is a pronoun; we do not use a noun after it.

Some children wanted to play football; others wanted to play computer games. (~~others children wanted~~)

The other can be used with uncountable and countable nouns, or with the pronouns *one* and *ones*.

There were two restaurants in the village.
*The first restaurant was closed, and **the other restaurant** was full!* (singular countable noun)
*Those books are Hilary's; **the other books** are mine.* (plural noun)

*This equipment belongs to us. **The other
equipment** over there belongs to a different
research team.* (uncountable noun)
*This water bottle is full. **The other one** is empty.
I don't like these shoes. I prefer **the other ones**.*

71 Passive voice

Forming the passive
The passive voice is formed by taking the
object of an active-voice clause and making it
the subject. The subject of the active clause
becomes the 'agent' (the 'doer') in the passive
clause and is indicated with the preposition *by*.
The passive verb is formed with *be* + past
participle.

Active
Subject   verb   object
*One of the students painted **this picture**.*

Passive
Subject   verb   agent
***This picture** was painted **by** one of the students.*

Using the passive
There are different types of situations where
the passive is normally used. The following are
frequent in academic English.

It-clauses
The passive is often used in *it*-clauses to refer
to what is common knowledge, to refer to other

people's work and ideas or to advance our own views.

It is often claimed that the state of the economy is the most important factor in how people vote in elections.

It has been shown that diet and general health are closely linked.

Indirect persuasion

The passive is often used in academic English as a way of indirectly presenting a judgement or opinion or persuading the reader or listener.

This research should be seen as a contribution to the debates about the role of motivation in language learning. (rather than *You should see this research as*)

After a noun

In academic English, a passive infinitive or a past participle with a passive meaning often follows a noun (underlined).

The conclusion to be drawn from these statistics is that the population was stable for more than 100 years. (= the conclusion which can/should be drawn)

The method chosen for the survey was a combination of interviews and questionnaires.

Using by + agent

It is not always necessary to use *by* and the agent. We do not need to state the agent when it is obvious and known to everyone.

Two men were arrested while trying to rob a supermarket yesterday. (we do not need to say *by the police*)

*The research **was carried out** over several months.*
(we do not need to say *by the researchers*)
See Get

72 Past perfect

The past perfect (*had* + past participle) is often used to give background information or reasons for other events in the past. It is not always necessary to use it when one event happens before another.
*I **forgot** to set the alarm on my phone and I **overslept**.* (the two events are presented as a sequence, one after the other)
*I **had forgotten** to set the alarm on my phone and I **overslept**.*
(the first event is presented as a background to or reason for oversleeping)

Pay
See Prepositions

73 People and person(s)

People is plural; it takes a plural verb.
***People are** always interested in scientific advances.*
Persons is a rather formal word which is often used in technical and official contexts.
(sign in a lift) *Maximum capacity 12 **persons**.*
The singular, *person*, is more neutral.
*Sally's a very nice **person**. I hope you get to meet her.*

Photograph
See Do and make

Point of view
See Opinion

74 Prepositions

Always check what the correct preposition is in a good dictionary. Here are just a few examples of common errors with prepositions.

About

Don't use *about* after words that should be followed by *of*. These include nouns such as *knowledge, impression, description, explanation, picture(s), photo(s).*
*You need a good knowledge **of** languages to apply for that job.* (~~knowledge about languages~~)
*What was your first impression **of** Matthew? Did you like him?* (~~impression about Matthew~~)
See Against

Above

When we refer to locations in relation to sea-level, we use *above*, not *over*.
*The lake is 1,000 metres **above** sea-level.* (~~over sea-level~~)

Against

Don't use *against* after *do something* when it means 'take action', for example to solve a problem.
*The government should do something **about** air pollution in our cities.* (~~do something against air pollution~~)

At

At is used when the speaker sees a time or a place as a point.

*It starts **at** six o'clock. I always go home **at** Christmas. It happened **at** midnight. I was tired **at** the end of the lesson.*
*I'll meet you **at** the station.*
*She's not **at** home.*
*There's a shop **at** the end of the street.*
See In and into
See On

By and until

Don't confuse *by* and *until*. *Until* means that something continues up to a point in time. *By* means that something must be done before that point in time at the latest.

*I have to submit my application **by** midday tomorrow.* (midday tomorrow is the latest time I can submit it)
*We have our hire car **until** next Friday.* (we have the car now and must return it next Friday)

Depend

The preposition that follows *depend* is *on*, not *of*.

*We might go to the beach. It depends **on** the weather.* (it depends of the weather)

Emphasise

Don't use *on* after the verb *to emphasise*.
*The president **emphasised** the importance of education in the development of the nation.* (emphasised on the importance)
We use *on* after the noun *emphasis*.

*The president placed great **emphasis on** the importance of education.*

For and during

We use *for,* not *during*, to talk about periods of time.

*We stayed in Helsinki **for** three days then took the ferry to Stockholm.* (~~during three days~~)

During can be used about events that happen when something else is happening.

*Somebody became ill **during** the lecture and they had to call a doctor.*

See Since

For + -ing

We use *for* with an *-ing* form to talk about how something is used.

*This website is very good **for finding** old school friends that you've lost contact with.*

We can also use *for* to talk about the reason for something.

*She was fined $300 **for stealing** a jacket from a clothes shop.*

*Her parents bought her a car **for doing** so well in her exams.*

When we talk about purposes or aims, we use the infinitive, not *for + -ing*.

*He's going to college in September **to study** social work.* (~~for studying~~)

For and since

For is used with a period of time. *Since* looks back to a point in time.

*We lived in Malaysia **for** two years in the 1980s.*

*I've been in my present job **since** 2002.*

See Since

In and into

Use *in* with parts of the day, months and seasons.

*Can we meet **in** the afternoon? I'm always very busy **in** the morning.*

*I'm going to Buenos Aires **in** November.*

***In** the summer we always go to the coast for a few weeks.*

If you are not sure, check in a good dictionary whether a verb should be followed by *in* or *into*. Here are some examples that often cause problems.

Verbs with *into*:

*She **came into** the room looking very sad.*

*The country is **divided into** four major regions.*

*I **moved into** my new flat last week.*

*She asked me to **translate** an email from Japanese **into** English.*

Verbs with *in*:

*We got **involved in** an interesting local history project.*

*Breakfast is not **included in** the price of the room.*

*His parents **invested in** a new online company about five years ago and became very rich.*

In front of and opposite

If you are standing *in front of* me in a queue of people in a shop, you will be served before me.

*The person sitting **in front of** me at the lecture was very tall, so I couldn't see the lecturer.*

If you are sitting *opposite* me in a restaurant,

we are facing each other.
The hotel is **opposite** *the main entrance to the railway station. You can't miss it.* (~~in front of~~)

Near and nearby

Use *near* as a preposition and *nearby* as an adjective or adverb.
We've booked a hotel **near** *the airport as our flight leaves very early in the morning.* (preposition) (~~nearby the airport~~)
During the lunch break, we went for a walk in a **nearby** *park.* (adjective)
She lives in Barton Street and her sister lives **nearby***.* (adverb)
This is a good rule of thumb, but don't be surprised if you occasionally hear people using *nearby* as a preposition.

On

We use *on* with days of the week, dates and important days in the year.
I'll see you **on** *Tuesday.*
They are arriving **on** *23rd April.*
On *New Year's Eve, we always have fireworks in our town.*
What are you going to do **on** *your birthday this year?*

Pay

If you *pay for* something you give money in order to receive it.
My uncle **paid for** *my birthday dinner last night.*
We don't use *for* with the word *bill* (the bill itself is free; you pay for the service listed on the bill)

*We have to **pay the bill** for the repairs to the roof by the end of the month.* (~~pay for the bill~~)

Reason
We say *reason for*, not *of*.
*What was the **reason for** their strange behaviour?* (~~reason of~~)
See Across, over and through

75 Present continuous

The present continuous is used for events and processes which are ongoing, where the start and endpoint are not important. We see the events from the inside looking outward.
*She **is working** for a software company at the moment.*
*I'**m writing** a novel, but I don't know if I will ever finish it.* (I am not writing it as I speak to you; it is an ongoing process)
If you want to talk about your birthplace or hometown or region, use the present simple; don't use the present continuous.
*I **come** from Hamburg.* (~~I'm coming from Hamburg~~)

76 Present perfect

We do not normally use the present perfect with expressions that refer to a definite time in the past (e.g. *last year, yesterday, in 1998*).
*I **moved** into this flat in 2011.* (~~I have moved~~)
We use the present perfect with time expressions which refer to periods leading up to now (e.g.

this week, since 2008, lately)
I**'ve lived** *in this house for ten years.* (i.e. the last ten years up to now)
When there is no time expression, we can use the present perfect to refer to events in the past which are still important or relevant now.
I**'ve bought** *a new guitar.* (I am not telling you when I bought it, but for me it's an important piece of news)
Use the present perfect, not the present simple, with the expression *the first time* when it means 'the first time ever', or 'the first time in my life'.
This is **the first time I've played** *in a band.* (~~the first time I play~~)

Progress
See Uncountable nouns

77 Pronouns with *-body* and *-one*

The following alternatives are all correct:
someone/somebody
anyone/anybody
no-one/nobody
everyone/everybody
The main difference is that the forms ending in *-body* are more common in speaking. The forms ending in *-one* are slightly more formal and are more common in writing.
Does **anybody** *have a pen I can borrow?*
No-one *likes to hear bad news.* (more formal)

Q

78   Quiet and quite

It is easy to confuse the spelling of these two words.

*They gave me a **quiet** room at the back of the hotel, which I liked.* (adjective: with little or no sound)

*The meal was **quite** good but it was not the best one I've had at that restaurant.* (adverb meaning 'fairly')

*I'm **not quite** ready yet. Can you wait five or ten minutes?* (adverb meaning 'not completely')

R

Regard
See Consider and regard

79   Relative Clauses

There are three main types of relative clauses. It is important to note the differences in the use of commas.

Defining
These are clauses that give essential information about a noun. In the examples below, taking away the underlined clauses leaves us with very little information about who or what is being referred to, or with something that means

something different.
Any student who fails the exam will have to re-sit it next term.
A car that was parked near the airport entrance was towed away by the police.
A man whose car was stolen a week ago was surprised to find it parked outside his house.
Defining relative clauses are not separated by commas.

Non-defining
These are cases where the information in the relative clause is extra. We can leave it out without changing the meaning of the main clause. Note the commas.
Auckland, which is New Zealand's largest city, has a population of around 1.5 million.
Julia, who was a very popular student, was elected to the student-teacher committee.

Sentential or comment
These are *which*-clauses that comment on a whole clause or sentence. Note the comma.
The meal cost £108 for two people, which is very expensive.
They lent us their flat for a week, which was very kind of them.
See Who, whom, whose, which, what, that

80   Remember, stop and try

Remember, try and *stop* can all be followed by an infinitive with *to* or by an *-ing* form, but the meaning is different in each case.

Remember

*Did you remember **to call** the electrician?* (i.e. I hope you did not forget)

*I remember **seeing** a car near the bank that morning, but I don't remember **seeing** anyone getting out of it.* (i.e. I saw a car but did not see anyone getting out of it. These are facts about the past)

Stop

*We stopped **working** at 5pm.* (i.e. we worked until 5pm)

*It was a long journey so we stopped **to have** lunch.* (we did not continue to travel, in order that we could have lunch)

Try

*I tried **to open** the door, but it was locked.* (I made an effort to open it but did not succeed)

Can you help me? My computer crashed. I tried **switching** it off and re-starting it, but it crashed again. (I switched it off to see if it would work, but it didn't)

S

81 Same and similar

The same is followed by *as*, not *than* or *that*.

*My phone is **the same** make **as** yours.* (same make ~~than/that~~ yours)

Similar is followed by *to*. It means 'like, but not identical'.

*When I move to Madrid, I'd like to get a **similar** apartment **to** the one I have right now.*

82 Say and tell

Say and *tell* have different grammar and a different meaning.

Say is used with a direct object and a prepositional phrase with *to*.

He **said something to me** that I didn't understand because he was speaking so quickly. (~~He said me something~~)

Tell is used with an indirect object (bold) and a direct object (underlined).

She told **me** she was leaving her job. (~~She told to me~~)

We use *say* when we want to focus on the words someone uses. We use *tell* when we want to focus more on the content or meaning of a person's words.

*I saw her in town yesterday. She looked at me, but she didn't **say** hello.* (~~she didn't tell me hello~~)

*I **told** him the names of some good restaurants in the city centre.* (I ~~said to him~~ the names)

83 Shall and will

When we refer to the future, *shall* can be used in formal situations with *I* and *we*.

*Providing my flight is on time, **I shall** arrive at 14:45.*

We shall *see what happens when the government brings in the new taxes.*

However, in everyday English, we can use *will* for all persons.

*I **will** contact you later in the week to confirm the time of the meeting.*

Shall is used to make suggestions with *I* and *we*.
***Shall we** get a takeaway tonight? I don't feel like cooking.*

84 Should

Should is used to express obligations or to give advice. It is less strong than *must* or *have to*.
*You **should** change the passwords you use for websites every so often.*
Should is used with *I* and *we* in very formal contexts instead of *would*.
*If you let me know when you are in Cambridge, I **should** be glad to meet you to discuss your plans.* (less formal: *I would be glad*)
See Must

Similar
See Same and similar

85 Since

Since is used to look back to points of time in the past.
*I haven't spoken to Rita **since** last Tuesday.*
Don't use *since* when you want to say how long something has lasted or taken. Use *for*.
*I've worked in this company **for** three years.* (~~since three years~~)
Since can also mean *'because'*. We normally use it at the beginning of the sentence.
***Since** it was very late, and the hotel restaurant was closed, we had to get room service.*
See For and during

86 Some and any

After a negative verb, we use *any*, not *some*, when we refer to an indefinite quantity.
A: *Do you need more chairs for the meeting?*
B: *No, thanks, we have enough. We **don't** need **any** more.* (We don't need some more)
In questions, *any* refers to an indefinite quantity, and usually, the speaker is not sure if the answer will be yes or no.
*Are there **any** restaurants near here?* (the speaker does not know if there are or not)
*It's one o'clock. Would you like **some** lunch?* (the speaker probably expects the answer to be yes)
We can use *some* after a negative verb if it means 'certain' or 'particular'.
*I **don't** know **any** of the people on this list.* (I know none at all)
*I **don't** know **some** of the people on this list.* (there are certain names, not all the names, that I do not know)

87 Still and yet

Still means that something is continuing, for perhaps a longer time than expected.
*I'm **still** waiting for a reply to my email to Lorna. I sent it three days ago.*
We use *yet* to refer to a period of time that comes up to the present, or that came up to a point in the past. It is typically used with a verb in the negative and in the present perfect or past perfect.

*I have**n't** had breakfast **yet**. Could you call me again in about half an hour?*

Note that in the examples, *still* comes after the auxiliary verb *am* and before the main verb; *yet* comes at the end of the clause. This is the most typical pattern.

Still normally comes between the subject and auxiliary or modal verb when the clause is negative.

*I **still** can't find my keys. I've searched everywhere!*

We can use *not yet* as a short answer.

A: *Has the post arrived?*

B: ***Not yet**.*

88 Street

We do not normally use *the* with the name of a street, except for *the High Street* (which usually means the main street in a smaller town or village). You can use *in* or *on* as a preposition. *On* is more common in American English.

*She owns a shop **in** Henry Street. (~~in the Henry Street~~)*

*Some shops **on** the High Street have closed down because of online shopping.*

89 Superlatives (biggest, best, most interesting)

After a superlative adjective used before a noun, we use *in*, not *of*.

*Auckland is **the biggest** city **in** New Zealand. (~~of~~*

~~New Zealand~~)

*He's **the cleverest** student **in** the class.* (~~of the class~~)

If there is no noun after the adjective, we can use *of*.

*James is **the oldest of** my three brothers.*

In the case of superlative adverbs, *the* is often omitted:

*Who can swim **(the) furthest**, you, your brother or your sister?*

90 Tags

There are three main types of tags in English.

*She's a teacher, **isn't** she?* (asking for confirmation – affirmative main clause, then negative verb + subject pronoun)

*You **don't** work on Saturdays, **do** you?* (asking for confirmation – negative main clause, affirmative tag)

*She's crazy, she **is**!* (used for emphasis – affirmative main clause, affirmative tag)

Take
See Bring and take
See Do and make

Tell
See Say

Than
See Comparative

91 That

That is used to introduce a clause acting as the object of verbs such as *hope, say, tell, reply, know, understand* (sometimes called reporting verbs).

*She **said that** she would help us to find an apartment.*

*We **knew that** something was wrong when David came running down the street.*

In less formal contexts, *that* is not necessary.

*They **said** the repair would cost £60.*

*I **know** you like Indian food, so I've cooked a curry.*

In formal writing, *that* can introduce a subject clause.

***That** the economy was weak in the 1990s is something which most economists accept.*

See Who, whom, whose, which what that
See Comparative

92 The

The English definite article is often difficult for speakers of other languages. However, there are some basic guidelines which may help.

The is used when the speaker/writer assumes that the listener/reader will understand which person or thing they are referring to. This may be for several reasons:

When the noun has already been mentioned

*There was **a little boy** standing at the door.*

*Nobody knew who **the boy** was, but he looked sad.*

When everyone knows the reference
The sun *was shining all day.*
Other examples: *the earth, the oceans, the sky*
When the listener/reader knows the reference
because it is shared with the speaker or familiar
*Shall we take **the kids** to **the park** after lunch?*
(the speaker expects the listener to understand
that this means 'our children, not somebody
else's, and that 'the park' is a place the speaker
and listener are familiar with)
Other examples: *the kitchen, the car, the
garden, the house, the microwave, the coffee-
cups, the living room*

**People, places, institutions which we assume
the listener/reader will interpret correctly**
*The Education Minist**er** is coming to our school
next week.* (the speaker assumes the listener
will understand 'the Education Minister of our
country, not that of some other country)
*I'll meet you outside **the Town Hall**.* (you will
understand which Town Hall I mean, probably
the one in our town, or in a town we are both
going to)
The university *is going to build some new
science labs.* (the university we both attend or
work at, or the university in our city, or in a city
we are talking about)
Other examples: *the government, the capital
city, the railway station, the campus, the
Ministry of Finance*

When not to use *the*
Don't use *the* when a noun refers to something
as a general idea or entity.

Money *is important, even if* **people** *say it isn't.* (money in general; all people) (~~The money ... the people~~)
I can't listen to **music** *and study at the same time.* (all or any music)
The music *in that film was fantastic.* (a specific example of music which the listener knows or will understand)
See Figures and tables

93 There is and there are

There is comes before a singular noun. *There are* comes before a plural noun.
If you need cash, **there is a bank machine** *in Milford Street and* **there is another one** *in the main square.*
There are *several good* **restaurants** *just around the corner from the hotel.*
However, in informal speaking, you will often hear people using *there's* with a plural noun. You should avoid this in formal writing.
There's a few problems *we need to solve before we can go any further.* (informal speaking; in formal writing, use *there are*)

Though
See Although, though, even though

94 Too, to, two

Don't confuse *too* and *to*. *Too* is used when there is more of something than is needed or wanted.

*This room is **too** warm. Shall I open the window?*
(~~to warm~~)
*I think 500 Euros is **too** much to pay for a hotel room for one night.* (~~to much~~)

When *too* means 'also', it normally comes at the end of the sentence.

*Joanna was at the party last night. Her sister was there **too**.*

In very formal situations, *too* can come between the subject and (auxiliary) verb.

*If you need further help, please contact Kerstin Holmbeck. She **too** is familiar with the situation and will advise you.*

The preposition and infinitive particle is *to*.

*She wanted to go **to** the cinema, but I didn't want **to**.* (~~didn't want too~~)

Be careful with the spelling of the number *two*.

*There were **two** police cars outside the bank yesterday.* (~~tow police cars~~)

95 Uncountable nouns

Uncountable nouns refer to things which, in English, are not counted as units, for example, *rice, milk, furniture, equipment, weather, information*. In many other languages, these can be counted and used in the plural. In English, uncountable nouns are not used with *a(n)* and not used in the plural.

Uncountable nouns can be used with other determiners and expressions of quantity such as *the, his/her, this, some, any, much, a lot*, etc. Here are some of the most common uncountable nouns that learners often have problems with.

Accommodation

In British English *accommodation* is uncountable.

*A lot of new student **accommodation** has been built near the campus.* (~~accommodations~~).
American English often uses it countably and you will see the plural *accommodations*.

Also note the spelling: two *c*'s and two *m*'s.

Advice

*My teacher gave me **some** good **advice**.* (~~a good advice~~ / ~~some good advices~~)
If you want to make a specific, individual reference, you can use *a piece of.*
*She gave me **a** useful **piece of advice** on how to do a good job interview.*

Damage

*The storm caused a lot of **damage** to people's homes.*

Damage can be used countably in the plural to mean financial compensation in a court case.
*Mr Roscoe was awarded £250,000 in **damages** in his libel case against a Sunday newspaper.*

Equipment

*The company makes scientific **equipment**.* (~~equipments~~)
If you want to make a specific, individual reference, you can use *a piece/piece(s) of* or *an item/item(s) of.*

*It was **a** complicated **piece of equipment** and it took me a long time to learn how to use it.*

Furniture

*We bought some new **furniture** for the living room. (~~furnitures~~)*

If you want to make a specific, individual reference, you can use *a piece/piece(s) of* or *an item/item(s) of.*

*Several valuable **pieces/items of furniture** from the old house were donated to the local museum.*

Homework

*The teacher often gives us **homework** to do over the weekend. (~~a homework~~ / ~~homeworks~~)*

Information

*We got some useful **information** from the Tourist Office. (~~informations~~)*

If you want to make a specific, individual reference, you can use *a piece/piece(s) of.*

*The document contained **a** valuable **piece of information**.*

Knowledge

*I gained some **knowledge** of physics by reading Stephen Hawking's books. (~~some knowledges~~)*

However, we can use *knowledge* with *a* when it is followed by *of.*

***A knowledge of** basic mathematics is important for almost any job these days.*

News

*I have **some** good **news** for you! (~~a good news~~)*

News is followed by a singular verb.

*The news **is** not good, I'm afraid.* (~~The news are~~)
If you want to make a specific, individual reference, you can use *a bit/bits of* or *a piece/piece(s) of.*
*She told me a few **bits of news** about her life recently.*

Progress
*You've made a lot of **progress** in your studies this year. Well done.* (~~progresses~~)

Research
*The team carried out major **research** from 2015 to 2018.* (~~a major research~~ / ~~major researches~~)
If you want to make a specific, individual reference, you can use *a piece/piece(s) of.*
*Their study was one of the most important **pieces of research** to be published last year.*

Travel
Travel refers to the idea of travelling in general.
*International **travel** is much cheaper these days because of low-cost airlines.*
An individual instance of travelling is *a journey* or *a trip. Journey* means the act of travelling from one place to another. *Trip* means the whole event of travelling, staying somewhere and returning.
*It was **a** long and tiring **journey**.* (~~travel~~)
*She has made three **trips** to Japan in the last 12 months.* (~~travels~~)
Travel can be used in the plural to refer to all the travelling someone has done.
*I've made a lot of friends in different countries in my **travels** over many years.*

*'Gulliver's **Travels**' is one of the most famous works of English literature.*

Weather

*What beautiful **weather**! Let's go to the beach today.* (~~what a beautiful weather~~)

If you want to make a specific, individual reference, you can use *a spell of.*

*We had **a spell of cold weather** at the end of the month and had to put on our winter clothes.*

Work

When *work* refers to the general idea of working, or to the place or time when you work, it is uncountable.

***Work** may not always be pleasant, but most of us have to do it to make a living.*

*What time do you start **work** tomorrow?*

Work which you do and get paid for is your *job.*

*I'm so bored here. I should look for a new **job**.* (~~a new work~~)

When *work* refers to art, it can be used countably.

*At School, we had to study some of Shakespeare's most famous **works** like 'Hamlet' and 'King Lear'.*

96 Very

We do not normally use *very* with adjectives which have extreme positive or negative meanings, such as *fantastic, amazing,*

marvellous, terrible, appalling. In these cases, we use *really* or *absolutely.*
It's an **absolutely fantastic** *film. I recommend it.* (~~very fantastic~~)
We enjoyed our holiday, even though we had some **really appalling** *weather.*

View
See Opinion

Wait for
See Expect, hope, wait for, wish

Weather
See Uncountable nouns

97 Weekend

British English speakers used to say *at the weekend*, but *on the weekend* is becoming more and more common. This is probably due to the influence of North American English.
What are you doing **at** *the weekend?*
What are you doing **on** *the weekend?* (becoming more common)

98 Who, whom, whose, which, what, that

Who, whom, which, whose and *that* are used in different types of relative clauses.
See Relative clauses

Who, that and whom (defining clauses)

Who and *that* are used in defining relative clauses (clauses which give essential information about a noun) when the subject of the clause is a person. *That* sounds slightly less formal.

The woman who/that played the guitar is from Mexico.

Who and *that* are also used when the object of the clause is a person.

*The student **who/that** I met was from Brazil.*

In more formal contexts, *whom* can be used when the object of the clause is a person.

*The student **whom** I met was from Brazil.*

Which and that (defining clauses)

Which and *that* are used when the subject of the relative clause is a thing or an idea. *That* sounds slightly less formal.

*The photograph **which/that** won the competition was taken in Finland.*

Which and *that* are also used when the object of the relative clause is a thing or an idea.

*The topic **which/that** the students chose for the debate was traffic pollution.*

Who, whom and which (non-defining clauses)

Who, whom and *which*, but not *that*, are used in non-defining relative clauses (clauses which give extra, non-essential information about a noun).

*The police, **who** arrived within minutes of the accident, closed the road to all traffic.* (~~that arrived~~)

*Charles, **whom** I had met briefly at a previous*

meeting, came over and said hello. (~~that I had met~~)

Which in sentential or comment clauses

Which is used in sentential/comment clauses.
*They let us stay in their flat, **which** was very kind of them.*

Whose (defining and non-defining clauses)

Whose is used to show possession.
*Students **whose** marks were below 50% were allowed to take the exam again.* (defining)
*The President, **whose** daughter accompanied him on the visit, arrived by helicopter this morning.* (non-defining)

Whose and who's

Don't confuse *whose* and *who's*. They are pronounced the same, but *who's* means 'who is'.
***Who's** coming to the party tomorrow?* (Who is coming ...?) (~~Whose~~)
***Whose** coat is this?* (Who does it belong to?) (~~Who's~~)

What

Don't use *what* in relative clauses.
*The car **that/which** I saw was dark blue, not black.* (~~The car what I saw~~)
What can be used to introduce subject clauses.
***What** we really need is somewhere to hang our coats.*

What and which in questions

When we ask a question with *what*, we are not thinking of a restricted number or set of things.
***What**'s your email address?* (open-ended; it could be any possible address) (~~Which is your email address?~~)

Which is used when we want someone to choose from a limited or restricted set of things. *There are six phone numbers in this list. **Which** number is yours?* (Which of the six?)

Wish
See Expect, hope, wait for, wish

99 Whole

We use *whole* to refer to things which are complete, or which are not seen as divided.
*She ate a **whole** pizza. I just had a slice.*
*When we arrived, the **whole** city was covered in thick smog.*
We can use a possessive determiner (e.g. *my, your, her*) before *whole*.
*She spent **her whole** life in the small village where she was born.*
When there is another determiner before the noun, we use *the whole of.*
*During **the whole of the** last decade, the country was not at peace for more than two years.*
Don't use *the whole* with uncountable nouns.
***All** the furniture was damaged in the fire.* (~~The whole furniture~~)

Will
See Shall and will

Work
See Uncountable nouns

100 Worth

The expression *to be worth* is followed by the
-ing form of a verb when talking about whether
something is a good idea or not.

A: *The train is very expensive. **Is it worth hiring***
a car instead? (~~worth to hire~~)

B: *No, **it's not worth spending** all that money.*
There are buses and they're much cheaper.
(~~worth to spend~~)

Worth can just be followed by *it*.

We thought about buying a new computer, but
*in the end, we didn't think **it was worth it** as we*
tend to use our phones for the internet these
days.

101 Your, you're, yours, yourself

Your and *you're* often sound the same when
pronounced, but don't confuse them. *Your*
indicates possession. *You're* is a short form of
you are.

*Is this **your** phone?*

*I hope **you're** enjoying your job.* (= you are
enjoying)

You're is only used with a verb in the *-ing* form
or the *-ed* form. Don't use it when there is no
other verb following it.

I wouldn't just go there if I were you. You should
*wait until **you're** invited.* (= you are invited)

*I'm looking forward to the dinner. I hope **you are***

too. (~~I hope you're too~~)

Yours indicates possession or a close relationship; it is a pronoun.

*I think this book is **yours**.*

*Is she a friend of **yours**?* (~~a friend of you~~)

At the end of a formal letter, use *yours*, not *your*, before *sincerely* and *faithfully*.

***Yours** sincerely, Frederica Conde* (~~your sincerely~~)

Yourself is written as one word.

*Did you hurt **yourself** when you fell off your bike?* (~~your self~~)

EXERCISES

If you are reading these exercises in the electronic version of this book, you may need to write or type your answers somewhere separately.

For the correct answers, see the key at the end of the exercises.

A Prepositions

What are the missing prepositions? If no preposition is needed, put X.

1   The government should do something _____ the pollution of our rivers.

2   What is the reason _____ the delay?

3   The teacher emphasised _____ the importance of learning a lot of new vocabulary.

4   We walked _____ the forest until we came to the main road again.

5   The village is 3,000 metres _____ sea level.

6   Rome is considered to be one of the most beautiful cities _____ the world.

7   Whether we go to the beach tomorrow depends _____ the weather.

8   They had a party _____ New Year's Eve.

9   We had to pay _____ a huge bill for repairs to our car last month.

10 The book contains some beautiful descriptions _____ the mountains and coastline.

11 You have to hand in your essay _____ 5pm on Friday. Next Monday is too late.

12 I have been in my present job _____ five years.

B Articles

Choose the correct answer: **a**, **an**, or **the**. If no article is necessary, put X.

1   Do you still use _____ laptop? All my friends just use their phones nowadays.

2   For most manual workers 100 years ago, _____ life was very hard.

3   I'll meet you at _____ station at two o'clock and we can both travel on _____ same train.

4   University fees are very high, and _____ students often have to get part-time jobs to survive.

5   Have you seen _____ TV remote control? I can't find it anywhere.

6   They had a meeting with _____ Minister of Education to discuss the national examinations.

7   I need _____ dictionary. Can I borrow one? There's ___ word I've never seen before in this text.

8   Please don't touch anything. The lab is full of _____ very expensive equipment.

9   Do you like _____ poetry? I've just read _____ beautiful poem about the sea.

10 Not every sentence in this exercise needs _____ article.

C Correct the mistakes

Each sentence has one mistake.

1 I decided to study child care at college. Because I've always wanted to work with children.

2 It's impossible to concentrate yourself when there is loud music in the background.

3 The temperature rose very slowly. See the below table.

4 My school always placed great emphasis in sports of all kinds.

5 I stayed with my cousin during three weeks last summer.

6 The country is divided in four major administrative regions.

7 There is a good hotel nearby the station. I can recommend it.

8 Can you wait a couple of minutes? I'm not quiet ready yet.

9 My bike is the same model than yours.

10 This room is to warm. Shall I open a window?

11 His wife got a baby last week so he's not at work this week.

12 That was a really good advice you gave me about interview techniques.

D Commas

Put commas where necessary in the sentences. Some sentences do not need any commas.

1   We bought some plates cups a coffee-maker and some cooking pots for our new flat.

2   The student who got the highest mark in the exam was from Brazil.

3   If you're looking for a budget hotel this is a good website.

4   The committee which consists of 12 members makes all the important decisions.

5   I'll tell Marcus about the rugby match when I see him tomorrow.

6   I left my hat and a scarf at your house yesterday. Can I come and pick them up?

7   The President who is 56 years old has three children.

8   There was heavy snow that day. As a result many flights were cancelled.

9   The person she admired most as a child was her geography teacher.

10 Latvia which is a member of the European Union has a population of just under two million.

E Choose the correct answer.

1   She did/made a lot of progress in her studies last year.

2   She is considered/regarded to be one of the greatest artists of her generation.

3   I love those sweaters, specially/especially the red one.

4   I expect/hope you have good weather for your holiday next week.

5   If/when I live till 100, I hope I will still be able to enjoy life to the full.

6   This tree loses all it's/its leaves in winter.

7   After we had bought the new furniture, there was few/little money left for other things.

8   That box looks very heavy. I help / I'll help you carry it.

9   I've got to know some nice persons/people at my evening class.

10 You need a basic knowledge about/of biology if you want to apply for the job.

11 She writes / is writing a book about India. She hopes to finish it by the end of this year.

12 [listening to music] This is the first time I hear / I've heard Swedish folk music. It's very beautiful.

F More on prepositions

Each sentence contains one incorrect preposition.
Correct them.

1   I'm moving in my new flat at the end of this month.

2   The Greek restaurant is nearby the museum in the
    main square; you can't miss it.

3   The price of crude oil has fallen in 20% over the last six
    months.

4   The accident happened at midday in the 23rd of April.

5   What was your first impression about our new
    Chairperson at the meeting yesterday?

6   There's an Italian restaurant in the end of the street
    which also serves a range of international dishes.

7   I've been living on the second floor of the building
    since two years.

8   The meal was expensive at that restaurant, and service
    was not included into the price.

9   Can you help me translate some of this German
    website about vegetarianism in English?

10 The art gallery is on the other side of the main square,
    directly in front of the town hall.

G Find and correct 10 mistakes in this text.

Students often find difficult to organise their personal finances. Not only they have to find affordable acommodation, they also have to pay for high rents and bills for electricity, heating, etc. The nowadays students typically have a part-time job, usually in hospitality industry. On the positive side, student loans are available, and students can lend money for their fees and personal expenses. On the contrary, this may mean they are paying their debts for a great amount of years after finishing their studies. Some universities and colleges offer scholarships; another universities offer reduced fees depending of the individual's financial circumstances.

Answer key to exercises

A Prepositions

If you got any of these answers wrong, go back and read the entries for the key words again.

1 about

2 for

3 X

4 through

5 above

6 in

7 on

8 on

9 X

10 of

11 by (*before* is also possible)

12 for

B Articles

1 a (laptop is a singular countable noun)

2 X (all life in general)

3 the (the station is known to the speaker and listener) / the (*same* needs *the* before it)

4   X (students in general)

5   the (the remote control is a familiar object for the speaker and listener)

6   the (the speaker and listener both understand which Minister they are talking about)

7   a (*dictionary* is a singular uncountable noun) / a (*word* is a singular uncountable noun)

8   X (*equipment* is uncountable)

9   X (poetry in general) / a (*poem* is a singular uncountable noun)

10   an (*article* is a singular uncountable noun)

C Correct the mistakes

1   I decided to study child care at college **because** I've always wanted to work with children. (not a new sentence – *because* gives the reason for the previous clause)

2   It's impossible to concentrate ~~yourself~~ when there is loud music in the background. (*concentrate* does not need a reflexive pronoun)

3   The temperature rose very slowly. See the ~~below table~~ **the table below**.

4   My school always placed great emphasis ~~in~~ **on** sports of all kinds.

5   I stayed with my cousin ~~during~~ **for** three weeks last summer.

6   The country is divided ~~in~~ **into** four major administrative regions.

7   There is a good hotel ~~nearby~~ **near** the station. I can

recommend it.

8   Can you wait a couple of minutes? I'm not ~~quiet~~ **quite** ready yet.

9   My bike is the same model ~~than~~ **as** yours.

10 This room is ~~to~~ **too** warm. Shall I open a window?

11 His wife ~~got~~ **had** a baby last week so he's not at work this week.

12 That was ~~a~~ really good advice you gave me about interview techniques. (*advice* is uncountable)

D Commas

1   We bought some plates, cups, a coffee-maker and some cooking pots for our new flat. (you will sometimes see a comma before *and* in sentences like this, but it is not necessary)

2   The student who got the highest mark in the exam was from Brazil. (no commas – defining relative clause)

3   If you're looking for a budget hotel, this is a good website. (subordinate clause 'If you're looking for a budget hotel' at the beginning of the sentence)

4   The committee, which consists of 12 members, makes all the important decisions. (non-defining relative clause, adding extra information – commas needed)

5   I'll tell Marcus about the rugby match when I see him tomorrow. (subordinate clause 'when I see him tomorrow' at the end of the sentence – no comma is needed)

6   I left my hat and a scarf at your house yesterday. Can I come and pick them up? (no comma needed before *and* in both cases)

7   The President, who is 56 years old, has three children. (non-defining relative clause, adding extra information – commas needed)

8   There was heavy snow that day. As a result, many flights were cancelled. (comma after sentence connector *as a result* at the beginning of the sentence)

9   The person she admired most as a child was her geography teacher. (no commas – defining relative clause)

10   Latvia, which is a member of the European Union, has a population of just under two million. (non-defining relative clause, adding extra information – commas needed)

E Choose the correct answer.

If you got any of these answers wrong, go back and read the entries for the key words again.

1   made

2   considered

3   especially

4   hope

5   If

6   its

7   little

8   I'll help

9   people

10   of

11   is writing

12   I've heard

F More on prepositions

If you got any of these answers wrong, go back and read the entries for the key words again.

1 I'm moving **into** my new flat at the end of this month.

2 The Greek restaurant is **near** the museum in the main square; you can't miss it.

3 The price of crude oil has fallen **by** 20% over the last six months.

4 The accident happened at midday **on** the 23rd of April.

5 What was your first impression **of** our new Chairperson at the meeting yesterday?

6 There's an Italian restaurant **at** the end of the street which also serves a range of international dishes.

7 I've been living on the second floor of the building **for** two years.

8 The meal was expensive at that restaurant, and service was not included **in** the price.

9 Can you help me translate some of this German website about vegetarianism **into** English?

10 The art gallery is on the other side of the main square, directly **opposite** the town hall. (it would be strange if the gallery was *directly in front of* the town hall)

G Find and correct 10 mistakes in this text.

Students often find **it** difficult to organise their personal finances. Not only **do** they have to find affordable **accommodation**, they also have to pay ~~for~~ high rents and bills for electricity, heating, etc. ~~The nowadays students~~ **Students nowadays** typically have a part-time job, usually in **the** hospitality industry [*industry* is a singular countable noun here]. On the positive side, student loans are available, and students can ~~lend~~ **borrow** money for their fees and personal expenses. ~~On the contrary~~ **On the other** hand, this may mean they are paying their debts for a great ~~amount~~ **number** of years after finishing their studies. Some universities and colleges offer scholarships; ~~another~~ **other** universities offer reduced fees depending ~~of~~ **on** the individual's financial circumstances.

TEN TIPS FOR ACADEMIC WRITING

1 Do not use informal language in formal writing (e.g. essays, dissertations, reports). For example, it sounds more formal to say, "We also carried out several interviews" instead of "We carried out several interviews as well". Another example is that students often overuse the verb *get*, as in "The more mass the object gets, the bigger it gets" (better to say, *The more mass the object acquires, the bigger it becomes*).

2 In formal writing, avoid contractions such as *it's, that's, we'll, they've* and write the words in full (*it is, that is, we will/shall, they have*).

3 Make sure you can use correctly words and phrases that are necessary time and time again to carry out typical functions in your writing. Keep a notebook of the ones you use most often. Here are some examples.

..., *as shown* in table 2 (not ~~as it is shown~~)

Such organisms are often found in the harshest environments. (not ~~Such kind of~~ ...)

First, I will survey the literature on the subject, secondly, I will outline the experiments carried out for this research and lastly/finally I will present the results and a discussion. (not ~~At first,~~ ... / not ~~at last~~)

4 Do not use the passive voice just to sound 'academic'. Read the entry on the passive voice in this book to see when it is most used commonly in academic writing.

5   Do not use *the* when referring to other specific parts of a text or particular items, for example, "See page 28" (not see ~~the~~ page 28), "Figure 2 shows the growth in population between 1994 and 2015" (not ~~The~~ Figure 2), "This will be discussed further in Section 4.1" (not ~~the~~ section 4.1).

6   Notice how tenses are used in academic writing. For example, if you consider someone's recent work to be very important or to have important consequences in the present, you may prefer to use the present perfect to refer to it:

*Wilson (2002) **has provided** us with a set of experimental guidelines which are still valid today.*

If the work is less important, or if it has been replaced by more recent work, you may prefer the past tense.

*Zarkov (2002) **listed** three criteria for this kind of investigation, but recently, these **have been revised** and reworked by Ahlev and Petersen (2017).*

7   Try to avoid being too direct and learn how to hedge (to make your statements and claims a little softer and less direct). Academic writers do this using verbs such as *suggest, indicate, claim, illustrate, point towards*, and by using modal expressions such as *may be, could be due to, perhaps, possibly, is likely*, etc. Compare these sentences:

*McCarthy (1998) **says** that vocabulary is the most important aspect of language learning.*

McCarthy (1998) **suggests/claims/proposes** *that vocabulary is the most important aspect of language learning.*

Discontent at work **is** *due to employees feeling undervalued by their employers.*

Discontent at work **is often due / may be due / is typically due** */ to employees feeling undervalued by their employers.*

8   Participle clauses are common in academic writing and can help you create a good academic style. Participle clauses used after a noun have either an active voice meaning (-*ing* clauses) or a passive voice meaning (-*ed* clauses). Here are some examples.

Active meaning

Parents <u>*attending school meetings*</u> *often complain about staff shortages.* (i.e. parents who attend)

Laws <u>*affecting the marine environment*</u> *are difficult to police.* (i.e. laws which affect)

Passive meaning

The method <u>*used in the study*</u> *proved to be very successful.* (i.e. the method which was used)

Goods <u>*manufactured overseas*</u> *are subject to a special tariff.* (i.e. goods which are manufactured)

9   Remember that a singular countable noun almost always needs a determiner of some sort. Determiners include words like *a(n), the, this, my, some, no.* Read the sections on *a(n)* and *the* in this book.

10 Make sure you know which of the most common nouns relating to aspects of academic English are countable and which are uncountable, especially the terminology of your discipline. Here are some general examples.

countable	uncountable
method	research
experiment	progress
survey	equipment
theory	transport(ation)
approach	accommodation
model	evidence
computer	leisure
analysis	knowledge
study	health

Always make a note whether the noun is countable or uncountable when you learn a new noun.

ABOUT THE AUTHOR

Michael McCarthy was born and grew up in Cardiff, Wales. He studied at Downing College, Cambridge from 1966 to 1973, where he received his MA and PhD. He later trained to be an English teacher at the University of Leeds.

He is Emeritus Professor of Applied Linguistics in the School of English, University of Nottingham, UK. He has also served as Visiting Professor in Applied Linguistics at the University of Limerick, Ireland, and Newcastle University, UK, and as Adjunct Professor at Penn State University, USA. He holds an Honorary Professorship at the University of Valencia, Spain. For the last 35 years, he has worked with large, computerised corpora of English texts, investigating them to establish how the vocabulary and grammar of English are used at the present time.

He is author/co-author of more than 50 books and over 100 academic papers dealing with the description and teaching of English, especially as a second or foreign language and with a focus on the spoken language. He has taught in Britain, The Netherlands, Spain, Sweden and Malaysia. He is co-author of the 900-page Cambridge Grammar of English, Grammar for Business, English Grammar Today and the globally successful Touchstone and Viewpoint courses for adult learners of English (all published by Cambridge University Press).

He has lectured in 46 countries on aspects of English and English teaching and has spoken about the English language in radio and TV interviews in different parts of the world.

A SELECTION OF BOOKS BY MICHAEL MCCARTHY

(2006) (With R. Carter) *Cambridge Grammar of English.* **Cambridge University Press.**

This is a major reference work (973 pages) covering all the important features of spoken and written grammar. It is based on seven years of research into corpora (large databases of spoken and written texts). It is also available with an optional CD-ROM.

http://assets.cambridge.org/97805215/88461/ frontmatter/9780521588461_frontmatter.pdf

(2007) (With A. O'Keeffe and R. Carter) *From Corpus to Classroom.* **Cambridge University Press.**

This book is aimed mainly at teachers of English and students of TESOL and applied linguistics interested in how spoken and written corpora can be used in language teaching. It covers subjects such as grammar, vocabulary (including idioms) and everyday interaction.

https://www.cambridge.org/core/books/from-corpus-to-classroom /035935BEDD0966BD83F1ED8BC58D8D3C

(2009) (with J. McCarten, D. Clark and R. Clark) *Grammar for Business.* **Cambridge University Press.**

A textbook for students of business English. In this book, the authors use evidence from a one-million-word corpus of business English to find the most common and useful grammatical features used in spoken and written business English. B1-B2 level.

https://www.cambridge.org/gb/cambridgeenglish/catalog/ grammar-vocabulary-and-pronunciation/grammar-business/

(2011) (with R. Carter, G. Mark and A. O'Keeffe) *English Grammar Today*. **Cambridge University Press.**

This is a comprehensive grammar reference book aimed at students and teachers of English. It covers spoken and written grammar and includes notes on common errors. The printed book has an accompanying workbook. The whole text is now also available to search and use free of charge online at

https://dictionary.cambridge.org/grammar/british-grammar/

(2012/2013) (with J. McCarten and H. Sandiford) *Viewpoint 1 and 2*. **Cambridge University Press.**

This is a two-level English course aimed at students who are moving from more general English towards academic, professional or vocational English. It is based on spoken and written corpora and is suitable for students at B2 to C1 levels. It is designed to follow on from *Touchstone* (see below).

https://www.cambridge.org/gb/cambridgeenglish/catalog/adult-courses/viewpoint

(2014) (With J. McCarten and H. Sandiford) *Touchstone. Student's Book. Levels 1-4*. **Second Edition. Cambridge University Press.**

Touchstone is a world best-selling four-level general English course taking students from A1 to B1 levels. It is based on corpus evidence, has dedicated lessons on everyday conversation strategies and a strong emphasis on vocabulary learning. The second edition is available in print, in blended format or completely online.

https://www.cambridge.org/gb/cambridgeenglish/catalog/adult-courses/touchstone-2nd-edition

(2016) (With F. O'Dell) *Academic Vocabulary in Use*. **Second edition. Cambridge University Press.**

As the title suggests, this book is aimed at students of academic English. It is a self-study textbook based on evidence from spoken and written academic corpora and consists of 50 units based around academic themes such as talking about cause and effect, presenting statistics, expressing opinions, etc. It also has a reference section and reading texts. It comes complete with an answer key.

https://www.cambridge.org/gb/cambridgeenglish/catalog/grammar-vocabulary-and-pronunciation/academic-vocabulary-use-2nd-edition/

(2017) (with Felicity O'Dell) *English Vocabulary in Use. Upper Intermediate*. **Fourth edition. Cambridge University Press.**

The globally successful *English Vocabulary in Use* series is now in its fourth edition at upper intermediate level. It has 101 self-study units covering a wide range of everyday topics (e.g. work, holidays, social media, health and medicine), and is based on spoken and written corpora. It also includes an e-book with audio.

https://www.cambridge.org/gb/cambridgeenglish/catalog/grammar-vocabulary-and-pronunciation/english-vocabulary-use-upper-intermediate-4th-edition

(2017) (with Felicity O'Dell) *English Idioms in Use. Intermediate and Advanced*. **Second edition. Cambridge University Press.**

These two self-study textbooks contain 60 and 62 units at B1-B2 and C1-C2 levels respectively, covering a wide range of topics and functions where idioms are used, for example, idioms relating to praise and criticism, danger, money, business, science, and so on. Based on spoken and written corpus evidence.

https://www.cambridge.org/gb/cambridgeenglish/catalog/
grammar-vocabulary-and-pronunciation/english-idioms-use-
intermediate-2nd-edition?format=PB

(2017) (with Felicity O'Dell) *English Phrasal Verbs in Use.*
Intermediate and Advanced. **Second edition. Cambridge**
University Press.

Along the same lines as the *Idioms in Use* books, these two
self-study textbooks contain 70 and 60 units at B1-B2 and C1-
C2 levels respectively, covering the grammar of phrasal verbs
and the different particles used (e.g. verbs with *in, out, up*).
A wide range of topics and functions is covered, for example,
agreeing, talking about numbers, decisions and plans, cause
and effect. Based on spoken and written corpus evidence.

https://www.cambridge.org/gb/cambridgeenglish/catalog/
grammar-vocabulary-and-pronunciation/english-phrasal-verbs-use-
intermediate-2nd-edition/

(2017) (with Felicity O'Dell) *English Collocations in Use.*
Intermediate and Advanced. **Second edition. Cambridge**
University Press.

Similar in style to the *Idioms in Use* and *Phrasal Verbs in Use*
books, these two self-study textbooks each contain 60 units at
B1-B2 and C1-C2 levels respectively, covering a wide range of
word-combinations commonly used in speaking and writing.
The topics and functions covered include current affairs,
fashion, thoughts and ideas, academic writing, etc. Based on
spoken and written corpus evidence.

https://www.cambridge.org/gb/cambridgeenglish/catalog/
grammar-vocabulary-and-pronunciation/english-collocations-use-
intermediate-2nd-edition/

(2019) *Grammar and Usage: Your Questions Answered*.
Cambridge: Prolinguam Publishing.

A new, updated version of Michael McCarthy's highly successful *English Grammar: Your Questions Answered* (2017). The book is aimed at native- and expert-users of English and gives advice on the most common problems people experience in grammar and usage in everyday speaking and writing.

e-book: https://amzn.to/2RiSGTP

paperback: https://amzn.to/2TFJPZ2

See Michael McCarthy's website for more information and a complete list of his publications.

http://www.profmikemccarthy.org.uk/

ACKNOWLEDGEMENTS

I am indebted to many colleagues in the ELT profession with whom I have worked over the years, too many to list here, but some have inevitably influenced me more than others. My first mentor was Amorey Gethin, with whom I worked in Cambridge in the early 1970s. Amorey was a most brilliant applied linguist; he helped me train myself to observe how learners learnt and what sorts of problems they encountered on the way. Together we collected field-notes of many of the common errors listed in this book. I also learnt a lot from my colleagues at KV Gothenburg, Sweden, during the late 1970s, particularly Mark Shackleton. On returning to the UK, I was privileged to work with some major figures in our profession throughout the 1980s at the University of Birmingham: John Sinclair, Malcolm Coulthard, Tim Johns, David Brazil, Michael Hoey, all of whom influenced me greatly. In the 1990s, I joined forces with the late Ron Carter at the University of Nottingham, and he will always remain my greatest colleague and co-author and my dearest professional friend. Norbert Schmitt, also at Nottingham, is another figure from whom I have drawn inspiration. Colleagues at Penn State, Valencia, Limerick and Newcastle must be added to the list, and, last but not least, my co-authors Geraldine Mark, Felicity O'Dell, Anne O'Keeffe, Jeanne McCarten and Helen Sandiford, who have provided me with invaluable insights that come from working closely with outstanding ELT practitioners.

This page has been left blank for you to make your own notes

_____

_____

_____

_____

_____

_____

_____

_____

_____

_____

_____

_____

_____

_____

_____

_____

_____

_____

_____

_____

_____

This page has been left blank for you to make your own notes

_____

_____

_____

_____

_____

_____

_____

_____

_____

_____

_____

_____

_____

_____

_____

_____

_____

_____

_____

_____

_____

_____

_____

_____

This page has been left blank for you to make your own notes

_____

_____

_____

_____

_____

_____

_____

_____

_____

_____

_____

_____

_____

_____

_____

_____

_____

_____

_____

_____

_____

_____

_____

_____

This page has been left blank for you to make your own notes

_____

_____

_____

_____

_____

_____

_____

_____

_____

_____

_____

_____

_____

_____

_____

_____

_____

_____

_____

_____

_____

_____

_____

This page has been left blank for you to make your own notes

_____

_____

_____

_____

_____

_____

_____

_____

_____

_____

_____

_____

_____

_____

_____

_____

_____

_____

_____

_____

_____

_____

Printed in Great Britain
by Amazon

poll tax
rebellion

danny burns

photographs by
mark simmons

First published by AK Press and Attack
International in 1992.

Text © Danny Burns
Photographs © Mark Simmons

Designed by Danny Burns
Cover design by Attack International
Cover photograph by Mark Simmons
Typeset by Fine Line Publishing Services

AK Press,
3 Balmoral Place,
Stirling FK82RD, Scotland.

Attack International,
BM 6577, London WC1N 3XX,
England.

British Library Cataloguing in Publication Data
Danny Burns
    Poll Tax Rebellion
        I.Title
336.220942
ISBN 1 873176 50 3

Dedication

To Susan – you supported me more than you know, thank you!

To everyone who refused to pay the Poll Tax. In particular to all those who were imprisoned for non-payment and for defending demonstrators against police attack.

To Sophie, for your love and support and all the time that we couldn't spend together - Mark

Acknowledgements

Photography and artwork
Mark Simmons
also Leon Kuhn, Rob Houn, Marea Angela Onofri.

For reading and commenting on the draft text
Paul Hoggett, Susan Bowers, Norman Blair, Alan Hirons, Alan Burns, Mike Vallance, Bob Goupillot, Allan Armstrong, Kenny Curtis, Dave Morris, Ian Greaves, Glen Burrows, Dave Chapple, Carol Burns.

For her tireless support throughout the campaign
Tessa Glinn.

Thanks also to
Ramsay Kanaan, Malcolm Imrie, Alistair Mitchell, Mike B, Paul Cook, Brian Slocock, Charles Wood, Steve West, Tim Puntis, Keith Miller, Caroline New, Tim Edgar.

Contents

Preface

This book is written as a tribute to a mass movement which defied the state and won. It is the story of ordinary people coming together in local communities to defeat injustice. It is not a tale of the heroic deeds of hardened political activists, for compared to the action and courage of ordinary people these pale into insignificance.

The aim of this book is to tell the story, as much as possible, in the voices of those who were involved. I have also tried to bring together some of the best photographs and graphics, which I hope convey something of the spirit of the movement. In the end, however, the book represents my view of events and takes a non-aligned position, as I did in the campaign.

Because I have felt it important to describe what happened in detail, a good proportion of the material is drawn from my experience of the South West of England. But I have also drawn heavily on detailed interviews and research which I carried out in Scotland and London, as well as material which has been sent to me from across Britain.

The book analyses what happened in the campaign, and speculates on the future of the left - because there are important lessons to be learnt. But I hope it will also be read as a story. The story of how the Anti-Poll Tax Unions were built; how the demonstrations grew into riots; how the court cases and the bailiffs were resisted; and ultimately how the tax was defeated by the sheer weight of non-payment.

There has never been a campaign of resistance in Britain which involved so many people in direct confrontation with the law. It was a historic event which gave hope to me and many others after the desolation of the Thatcher years. Such mass-resistance is surely the route to creating a just society.

Danny Burns, January 1992.

1

A HATED TAX

The Poll Tax was a flat rate tax. It was not based on ability to pay. Everyone over eighteen was liable. Rich and poor paid the same. The millionaire paid the same as the toilet attendant. The lawyer paid the same as the shop assistant. The Prime Minister Margaret Thatcher and her multi-millionaire husband paid the same as their gardener.

The tax, officially called the Community Charge, was dubbed the Poll Tax because of its similarity to a tax introduced in 1381. That tax was so disliked it provoked the peasants' revolt. The government tried to counter this analogy, but the name stuck.

The effects of the Poll Tax were devastating. Many people had to pay bills which were two or three times higher than before. This was because the costs of administration were twice as high and because dramatic reductions in the tax bills of the wealthy were paid for by ordinary people. Examples like this one reported in *The Guardian* newspaper made people furious:

> The Duke of Westminster, who used to pay £10,255 in rates on his estate has just learned his new poll tax: £417. His housekeeper and resident chauffeur face precisely the same bill.

Even though the Poll Tax was heavily subsidised in the first year (to cushion the government against political dissent during the period of implementation), it was still too much for millions of ordinary people to pay.

With a confidence which came from three general election victories, the government openly defended policies which widened the gap between rich and poor. They argued that if there were no differentials between people, there would be nothing for people at the bottom of the ladder to aspire to. This perspective was reflected in their analysis of the Poll Tax:

> Why should a duke pay more than a dustman? It is only because we have been subjected to socialist ideas for the last 50

years that people think this is fair.
Nicholas Ridley, Environment Secretary, 1/4/88.

This 'socialist idea' which Ridley referred to was the welfare state. A system which while imperfect was nevertheless based on the fundamental principle that everyone should have basic human rights to good health care, educational opportunities, decent housing, and a reasonable standard of living. In the past the Tories had paid lipservice to these rights to keep the lid on dissent. But by 1979, they felt confident enough to abandon such concessions, believing that as long as the majority of people were better off they would continue to vote Tory. Given this, it didn't matter if conditions for the bottom third of the population degenerated. The Poll Tax, an overt and undisguisable redistribution of wealth from the poor to the rich, symbolised this major change in Tory thinking.

It was invented by the radical Right think-tank, 'The Adam Smith Institute', which was ironic because Adam Smith had explicitly rejected the idea over 200 years ago:

A Poll Tax on free men is either altogether arbitrary or altogether unequal, and in most cases is both the one and the other.
Adam Smith, The Wealth of Nations, 1880.

The only other country in the world which had a Poll Tax – Papua New Guinea – was in the process of abolishing it. Despite warnings that the Poll Tax would be a political and administrative disaster from virtually every professional institute, and even members of the cabinet, the government pressed on with a time-table which would see the tax introduced in Scotland by April 1989, and in England and Wales a year later. They mounted a massive propaganda campaign, asserting that it would make local government more accountable, and that the taxation system would be more efficient and fairer!

Thatcher argued that everyone should pay something towards local government because

11

it was only if people's own money was being spent that they would care enough to vote against high-spending Labour councils. But virtually everyone already had a stake in local services because most of those who didn't pay rates directly, were either married women, who in practice paid rates as part of a household (even if their husbands actually paid the bill), or were the poorest members of the community who needed council services and who therefore had a strong interest in ensuring that money was not wasted. In any case, this argument about accountability was hypocritical because the Poll Tax capping procedure meant that the government could limit the amount local authorities could raise through local taxation if, in their view, councils were spending too much. So the local electorate could vote for taxes to come down and services to be cut, but they couldn't vote for taxes to go up and services to be expanded. It was not 'coincidental' that all of the councils capped in the first year were Labour controlled.

The rich get richer,

the poor poorer, and the

councils continue to

administer the process.

Not only did the legislation restrict the rights of democratically elected councillors to follow the mandate they were elected on but, for the first time, the government appointed

un-elected officers of the council (Community Charge Registration Officers) with powers to over-ride decisions made by elected council-lors. They also introduced a register (of people liable to pay the tax) which raised many ques-tions about civil liberties:

> The public register would need extensive support files. Behind the register there will have to be a second file recording the notes, anecdotes and suspicions the Au-thority has about individuals.
> *Chartered Institute of Public Finance Accountants quoted in NCCL Civil Liberty briefing, No.7, January 1988.*

The register was to be a mechanism of social control. It required people to register their whereabouts every time they moved. Many feared that this was a prelude to national iden-tity cards. Serious concern was also expressed about the use of the electoral register to compile the lists for the Poll Tax register. It was clear from the start that huge numbers of people would not be able to pay and, in order to avoid being tracked down, would not register to vote. Since those who were least able to pay were most likely to vote Labour (if they voted at all), it was in the Tories' interest to disenfranchise them. An article in *The Guardian* later con-firmed people's worst fears:

> More than one million voters have disap-peared from the electoral register since the Poll Tax was conceived... The number of teenagers registering in advance of their 18th birthday fell last year by 11%. The analysis by the Office of Population Census and Surveys will strengthen the belief that people have deliberately not placed them-selves on the electoral register in the hope of escaping liability for the Poll Tax.
> *The Guardian, 19/6/91.*

Despite all this, the main argument against the Poll Tax was that it was blatantly unfair. It was like Robin Hood in reverse: stealing from the poor to give to the rich. In the words of a

13

Bristolian interviewed outside the Poll Tax courts:

> They ask for all this money, and at the end of the day, they don't want us taking no more big pay rises or nothing like that, yet yesterday all the top people they got nice big pay rises and they can afford to pay it anyway. So at the end of the day we're left with no money. They're just trying to rob us blind. If we did anything like that, went out and robbed someone, you'd be straight in court wouldn't you... It ain't fair.
> *Terry Francis, 1/2/91.*

The government argued that because everyone used services everyone should pay for them. Of course they deliberately ignored the fact that many local council services (such as subsidised housing and social services) are needed precisely because people have no money. The argument that everyone should pay the same might of course have some validity if everyone was paid the same – a perspective unlikely to be adopted in a capitalist society. In any case, the Tories' argument was undermined by the fact that they applied it so selectively:

> If this is such a good principle how come it isn't being applied to Northern Ireland? Any volunteers for tracking down non-payers? And if the principle that people should pay for the services they consume, irrespective of their ability to pay, is right, then how come it hasn't been applied to income tax as well? I offer this as a free gift for the next Conservative Party manifesto. Add up the revenue from income tax and divide it by the number of people on the electoral register and charge it at a flat rate to reflect the undoubted fact that we all get similar benefit from spending on defence, roads, education, etc. Then light the blue touch paper and withdraw.
> *Victor Keegan, The Guardian Economic Notebook, 26/3/90.*

14

Their principled arguments in tatters, the government began to suggest that the burden of taxation was really on income tax payers:

> The Community Charge is related to people's ability to pay, as about half of local government spending is paid for by central government from tax payers' money, and to this sum the higher tax payers have contributed proportionately more. Just over a quarter comes from business ratepayers. It is only the domestic ratepayers' share which is going to be met from the Community Charge.
>
> *Jonathan Sayeed, Conservative MP, Bristol East, standard letter to constituents, 1989.*

But, in suggesting that income tax was progressive, they failed to mention that since 1989 they had massively reduced the top rate of income tax from 87% to 40%. They also tried to cover up the effects of the Poll Tax by suggesting (through a multi-million pound advertising campaign) that it was accompanied by a comprehensive rebate scheme. Yet a single person could earn as little as £75 a week after tax (around £4,000 a year) and still not get a rebate. If she lived in parts of London, where the Poll Tax was as much as £500, she could be expected to pay as much as an eighth of her income on local taxation – a huge amount for someone who earns only £75.

In 1991, the average manual worker received only £242 per week before tax; many got far less (the average part-time female manual worker, for example, earned only £64.40 for an 18.5 hour week) before tax. Couples with children often only had one income and probably a high rent or mortgage to pay out of this, yet both partners had to pay the tax. This poverty trap applied to large numbers of people. In fact, repeated surveys indicated that more than 70% of the population would be worse off under the Poll Tax.

Campaign groups and advice centres were inundated with tragic stories about the plight which ordinary people faced:

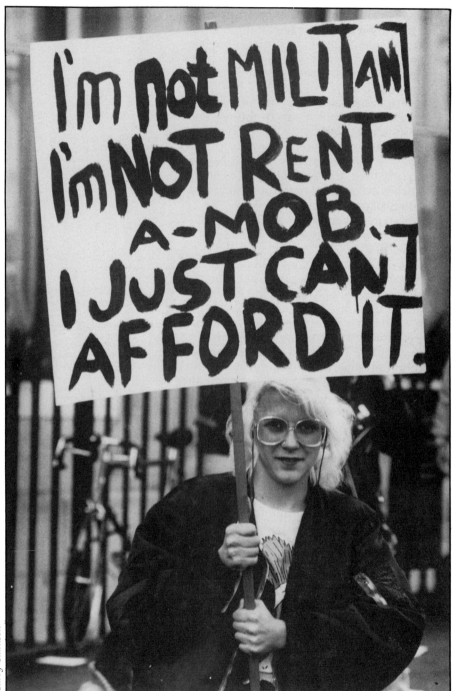

Garry Clarkson

We are a single income couple who have
been refused rebate as we are a few
pounds over the limit. This is causing severe
hardship. We have two children under five
and it is food we are cutting back on. It will
mean doing without heating in the winter.
Church Action on Poverty, Survey, 1990.

Tower Hamlets resident Abdul Khalid is
married with five children. He earns £90 a
week as a cook. He pays £37 a week in rent
and £10 a week for school meals. Tower
Hamlets has a liability order against him
and his wife – their combined Poll Tax bill
£594, but with court and bailiff costs the
council is seeking £836.
LGIU, Poll Tax focus, No.16, February, 1991.

With a few minor exceptions, such as the
'severely mentally impaired', members of reli-
gious communities and the homeless sleeping
rough, there were no exemptions. Even those
on income support receiving only £30 week
(and those under 25 who had recently had their
income support cut to £26 a week) still had to
pay 20%. Many people pleaded to the government for help. One 83-year old pensioner from
Milton Keynes, who with her husband faced an
increase from £422 to £797 wrote to her MP to
point out that her Poll Tax took fourteen weeks
of her entire pension. She asked for suggestions
as to how she should live during those weeks.
Her letter was ignored (Church Action on Poverty, 1990).

Some sections of the community were particularly vulnerable. Tenants in private rented
accommodation were effectively being asked
to pay their local taxes twice. In the past, the
rates had been charged as part of their rent
payment to landlords, who then took out the
relevant amount and paid it to the council.
After the introduction of the Poll Tax, when
landlords no longer had to pay this money,
very few landlords agreed to put the rent
down, and tenants had no legal right to enforce
a reduction. It was estimated that by January
1990 Scottish landlords had made about £40

*Opposite: The government
tried to label those opposed
to the Poll Tax as
extremists, but as early as
1987 ordinary people were
taking to the streets to
demonstrate their anger.*

million by capitalising on this. In England and Wales, it was expected that they would make over £100 million (*The Observer*, 2/8/90).

As Mike Reardon of the Association of Metropolitan Authorities pointed out, 'Asking people with tenancies to confront landlords about rent reductions is asking them to get themselves thrown out of their homes.' (23/1/90). This is the story of a couple in Norfolk:

Above:

Even pensioners had to pay

the Poll Tax if they lived

with their families, but they

didn't have to pay if they

lived in a home!

The Tories only seemed to

believe in the family when it

suited them.

> My wife and I are tenants who paid £260 in rates last year as part of our rent. There has been no reduction since April 1990. The house owner is keeping the extra amount as a rent increase. The Poll Tax, therefore, increases our bills by £682 per year. We have a tenancy agreement that is, by law, terminated and renegotiated every six months. If we disagree with the owner about the rent we could be evicted very easily. We cannot afford to buy a house and there is no possibility of us obtaining a council house.
>
> Church Action on Poverty, 1990.

People from ethnic communities, many of whom lived in large extended families, were hit particularly hard. They often had grown-up children living at home in cramped conditions.

Whereas before they had to pay one bill for the household, now they had to pay for every individual.

Student nurses were also badly hit. At the 1990 Annual Conference of the Royal College of Nurses, Virginia Bottomley, the Health Minister, had to face a barrage of anger from members of a traditionally moderate union:

> Would you explain why the majority of student nurses have to pay 100% of Poll Tax but trainees in the Armed forces on salaries of up to £9,500 pay only 20%?'
> Maybe the difference is that you epitomise a government which cares more about the people it employs to kill other people.

Stories like this flooded both the national and local media. One minute the focus was on the nurses, next on the disabled, then on the pensioners. For many the Poll Tax was the last straw. The cushioning from the welfare state had been substantially eroded; education was being reduced to vocational training in ageing schools; the health service was falling apart; there was a chronic shortage of housing and unemployment had rocketed. The cumulative effect of these changes had made conditions intolerable. A 1991 report on poverty highlighted the degree of inequity which had resulted from ten years of Thatcherism:

> More people are living in relative poverty in the United Kingdom than in any other European Community country. One in five of all EC residents defined by the Commission as poor lives in the UK, says the report which examines spending figures for each member state. Measured by family group the findings are even more stark. Almost one in four of all EC households defined as poor is in the UK. The report... also suggests that the UK's record has worsened dramatically while the EC as a whole has kept the growth of poverty at bay.
> *Report from second European Poverty Programme, The Guardian, 8/4/91.*

19

Living standards for ordinary people had plummeted. For some it was quite literally the end of the road:

> A pensioner barricaded himself into his flat in Bedford and burned himself to death after scrawling on a bedroom wall the words 'barbaric Thatcherism killed me.'
> He died at the Stoke Mandeville hospital in Buckinghamshire, and the inquest at Aylesbury heard that Mr. Joe Newman, aged 66, a former Polish prisoner of war, had walked around Bedford town centre carrying a placard proclaiming 'I survived Stalin and Hitler, but I will not survive the way Thatcher treats pensioners.'
> *The Guardian, 17/3/90.*

Thatcher's victories in the 1980s were notable for two things: their careful planning (during the 1985 miners' strike, for example, coal had been stockpiled for over a year before the set piece confrontation) and the way that she picked off her targets one by one (enlisting the support of the rest of the population to legitimise what she was doing). As a result, she was able to tame the trade union movement, decimate local government and abolish the GLC, one by one. The official parliamentary opposition, after ritual denunciation of every new Thatcher attack, meekly accepted everything she implemented. But, in her third term of office she began to show less restraint. With the Poll Tax she took on the whole population.

> The government has declared war on the people.
> *Anthony Marlow, Conservative MP for Northampton, March 1990.*

This was her biggest mistake.

2

PROTEST OR
RESISTANCE?

Rob Houn

Scotland: A Strategy Unfolds

While the vast majority of people opposed the Poll Tax, there was no agreement on how to challenge it. Between the middle of 1987 and the end of 1988 the Scottish people lined up behind different strategies. Members of the Labour Party and TUC opted for a protest campaign to put pressure on the government not to implement the Poll Tax. But many in the local communities, the neighbourhoods and the Scottish housing schemes believed that protest would never be enough – that a campaign of resistance needed to be organised. This chapter documents the struggle between these positions – a confrontation between the poorest people of Britain and those who claimed to represent them.

In early 1987, the Labour Party announced a campaign called 'Stop It'. Using tactics which ranged from petitions and legal challenges to information briefings, they sought to change the climate of public opinion and put pressure on the government. Their aim was to stop the Poll Tax before it was implemented:

> It would seem to me appropriate for all those opposed to the Poll Tax to unite under the banner of the 'Scottish Campaign Against The Poll Tax'. They aim to stop the introduction of the Poll Tax and that clearly should be everyone's objective. To simply give up the fight to stop the introduction of the Poll Tax and call for a boycott as your organisation does, appears to me to be defeatist.
> *Danny Crawford, Glasgow City Councillor to Susan Hay of the Anti-Poll Tax Union, November 1987.*

Many prominent Labour activists believed that it would be possible to stop the tax simply by voicing their opposition. Given the history of failed confrontation with the government (particularly the battles over rate capping and the abolition of the GLC), this seemed extremely naive. On the other hand, it is certain that central Labour strategists knew that they had no chance of forcing a withdrawal of the Poll Tax before a general election, and it was to their electoral advantage to see the Tories flounder while trying to implement it. The Labour Party project throughout the 1980s had been to make themselves 'electable'. It continued to be their central preoccupation throughout the campaign:

> This is a party that aspires to be in government. Our aim is to redress the balance in the interests of ordinary people. I don't believe such a party can afford selective amnesia when it comes to the law of the land.
> *Donald Dewar, Labour MP, Shadow Scottish Secretary, 17/9/88.*

The Labour Party leadership feared to cross the line of 'legitimate' protest because they hoped to be in government in the future, and they expected their own laws or policies to be obeyed. They thought it folly to undermine a parliamentary democracy which had been fought over for many centuries – a system which they saw as redressing inequalities in society, and so they rejected a campaign to break the law. But they also knew that they had to be seen to be doing *something*. A propaganda campaign which didn't challenge their newly respectable image was the only way these objectives could be combined.

The 'Stop It' campaign produced posters, leaflets and stickers, had letters published in the press and its leading light, the MP Brian Wilson, made speeches challenging the fairness of the Poll Tax. But, in its first year, the campaign did little more than that. Its one serious initiative was the 'send it back' campaign, which told activists to return the registration forms and ask awkward questions of the council officers. Its aim was to delay the system and to make 'a legitimate protest'. Unfortunately, not only was this tokenistic (because the Labour Party very quickly recommended that people register), it was also flawed, because it meant that thousands of people were volunteering basic information, such as their names and addresses, which could be used against them later when they were chased up for non-payment.

At about the same time, an informal grouping called 'Citizens Against The Poll Tax' formed a non-party political protest campaign. Unlike the Labour Party, their campaign aimed to challenge the implementation of the Poll Tax. They suggested that people 'from local groups take part in fun/fundraising activities' in order to raise money for publicity, but they didn't campaign for local groups as centres of resistance. Their emphasis was on letters to prominent politicians and symbolic action:

> On the day the local registration officer starts compiling his register, try to get as many local people as possible to take part in a symbolic 'sleep out' or all night vigil in some public place so that nobody will be home that night.

Citizens Against The Poll Tax were widely seen as:

> ... a sort of irate, largely middle class element who... just seemed to hang around, they never really got involved with the people who were trying to build the local groups... they had letters in *The Scotsman* and things like that... they used publicity, that was the way they operated.
> Bob Goupillot, Community Resistance Against The Poll Tax, 3/5/91.

They were fairly successful at getting publicity for the Anti-Poll Tax cause, but because their campaign was mainly based on providing information they failed to mobilise large numbers of people. Nevertheless, while they acted wholly within the law, they refused to condemn civil disobedience (seeing it as a mat-

Marea Angela Onofri

ter of individual conscience). In the early days of the campaign, they sent information to every Anti-Poll Tax group, including those working outside the law. They also compiled a register of 'those... prepared to take such a stand'. But in offering support to non-payers they seemed to have little appreciation that for many it wasn't a matter of choice. This could be seen as an outcome of their mainly middle class base, where conscience was a more important political motivation than economic necessity.

Real resistance to the Poll Tax began after 'The Community Charge Bill for Scotland' received the royal assent in May 1987. Ironically, it didn't come from any of the major organisations who were to play key roles in the non-

Above: A Scottish piper

plays the non-payment

tune to a growing

campaign.

payment campaign. A small political grouping – The Workers Party of Scotland – organised a series of meetings in Glasgow. They set up an organisation called 'The Anti-Poll Tax Union'. Its aim was to co-ordinate resistance to the Poll Tax across Scotland. Two of its key activists, Paul Cockshott and Matt Lygate, organised a

march from Glasgow to Aberdeen. They visited people throughout Scotland and handed out a pamphlet they had written in April called 'The Poll Tax Nightmare'.

The programme set out by the Anti-Poll Tax Union in early 1987 was very similar to that later adopted by the movement as a whole in early 1988 (and 1989 in England and Wales).

Above:

The long march from

Glasgow to Aberdeen.

Their aim was to 'make Scotland a country free from the Poll Tax'. They saw the Poll Tax as the imposition of an illegitimate British law on the people of Scotland. The Anti-Poll Tax Union strongly emphasised the need to build networks in order to 'bring the support of one area to another'. They also stressed the importance of information, pledging to produce 'masses of leaflets, posters, stickers etc. and to display and distribute them throughout Scotland'. Their campaign was to be locally organised in the neighbourhoods and the housing schemes. This was the first mention of a grass roots campaign which involved talking with people, an approach which contrasted strongly with Labour's 'paper' campaign.

This local approach was first put into practice in the Maryhill area of Glasgow. A local Anti-Poll Tax Union was formed in April 1987. Members of the union went round the houses and talked to people and, by January 1988, the union had over 2,000 paid up members:

> They were the first people to go round the doors. They took these cards round the doors and asked people to pay a donation and pledge themselves to non-payment.
> *Allan Armstrong, Chair, Lothian Federation APTUs, 6/5/91.*

The Anti-Poll Tax Union was also the first group to organise for non-payment, and it was on this basis that people were called on to join the union:

> This is a direct appeal from the people of Maryhill/Summerston to the workers in this area. Please help us, we are the large families, the unemployed and the pensioners. This is a cry from the poor who need you and your support... We have formed a branch of the Anti-Poll Tax Union in the Maryhill/Summerston area who are campaigning against this taxation and calling for non-registration and non-payment in protest against this tax.
> *Letter from the Anti-Poll Tax Union to local workers, May 1987.*

The Maryhill Anti-Poll Tax Union didn't last long. While it retained a strong core of non-payers it was unable to sustain its organisational base. Nevertheless, the non-payment platform it put forward, and its focus on local grass roots organisation, set the strategic agenda for the Anti Poll Tax movement over the next three years. It also provided the name 'Anti-Poll Tax Union' which was adopted by most of the local groups in the campaign.

After Maryhill, the focus switched to Edinburgh. In September, the Workers Party of Scotland, along with the Revolutionary Democratic Group (an offshoot of the Socialist Workers Party), set up a local Anti-Poll Tax group in Leith which ran weekly stalls outside the local shopping centre. This was the first Anti-Poll Tax Union to have a continued existence throughout the campaign. Over the next months a group was set up in Stockbridge New Town. This very quickly grew too big and was split to form the Broughton/Inverleith Anti-Poll Tax group. Soon after, groups were set up in Prestonfield, Armdale, Newhaven/Fort, Sciennes/Marchmont, Abbeyhill and Gorgie/Dalry.

A general call for resistance was made in the autumn of 1987 by a coalition of different organisations. The key ones were 'Community Resistance Against The Poll Tax' (libertarian socialists) and the Militant Tendency (on the Left of the Labour Party), although other organisations such as the Revolutionary Democratic Group also played a role. They had different motivations and traditions but were

united in a belief that protest was not enough. The importance of these groupings should not be underestimated, nor the debates which they were engaged in, because, in the absence of the organised labour movement, they provided the political and intellectual ideas which underpinned the resistance strategy. As the movement grew and ordinary people began to outnumber the political activists, their tactical influence diminished, but their strategic influence continued to set the agenda.

Their call for resistance differed from the protest calls because its purpose was not solely to express personal morality or to influence opinion but rather to influence events. The actions taken would have a direct impact on the outcome of the struggle and would not be dependent on the results of elections. Resistance meant confrontation. Advocates of resistance believed that the Anti-Poll Tax campaign needed to be built on a direct challenge to implementation, not the false hope that someone might agree not to implement it.

In the past, campaigns of resistance have included non-co-operation; pickets and strike action; occupations; harassment and sabotage. These have been complemented by demonstrations and other forms of protest in order to create an atmosphere of resistance and build inspiration for action. Modern democracies depend on majority support for a mandate to

Craig McLean

Above:

Members of the

Prestonfield group -

some of the first Anti-Poll

Tax activists.

rule, but they depend on the compliance of a much larger majority to maintain order. If serious dissent reaches more than about 10% of the population then there either have to be concessions or the conflict has to be escalated through serious repression. It is for this reason that resistance can have such a direct impact on change.

The activists who called for resistance came from a different background to most of those arguing for protest or civil disobedience. Many of those involved with 'Community Resistance' were unemployed and had previously been involved with the Unemployed Workers' Centre and Claimants' Union in Edinburgh. The tradition of these activists was self-organisation. Nobody had ever represented them or given them resources in the past, so they had developed techniques of organising outside the official structures. Their philosophy was broadly socialist, but anti-state and not centralist. Their name reflected their community–based approach:

It called itself 'Community Resistance'
because it mainly started off doing solidarity work against South African apartheid,
and it was called Community Resistance in
recognition that it was the communities in
South Africa where the revolt was taking
place.

Bob Goupillot, Prestonfield and District Community Resistance
Against The Poll Tax, 3/5/91.

This tradition was an important influence on
the way the local groups later developed. A
Glasgow Evening Times article (21/3/91)
showed how it was put into practice:

Using tactics modelled on the South African
townships, many areas have become no-go
areas for sheriff officers with literally hundreds of pairs of eyes on the look-out.

Community Resistance activists rebelled
against the bureaucratic models of organisation inherited from the labour movement, these
were seen as exclusive and alienating. Their
focus was on talking to people and 'doing
things' at a local level. They took political inspiration from anarchist and autonomist direct
action in Spain and Italy, self-organisation
characterised by squatters in London, Berlin
and Amsterdam, and the 1968 uprising in
France. They stressed the importance of the
movement being non-aligned, believing that if
the campaign was directly linked to a particular party, faction or organisation, vast numbers
of people would not get involved. They felt
that the movement should be a reflection of the
views of local people, so they emphasised the
involvement of people who had never been
involved in organised politics before. This led
them to distance themselves from the leaders of
the labour movement and, unlike other groups,
they refused to call on the labour movement to
lead the Anti-Poll Tax movement.

Militant activists came from a different
background. Many of their supporters in Scotland lived on the most run-down housing
schemes. Of all the Left groupings they had by

far the strongest working class base. Their political inspiration was more closely linked to the history of struggle in Glasgow and the rent strikes of 1915. Militant's involvement is interesting because they had no real history or experience of working outside traditional structures. But with the growth of 'designer Labourism', and the expulsion of leading Militant activists, their scope for manoeuvre within the Labour Party was extremely limited. This meant they had to build a new political base.

Militant eventually dropped much of their Labour Party activity to concentrate on the Anti-Poll Tax campaign but this didn't happen automatically. It was only once Russell Taylor (a prominent Militant activist in Edinburgh) got involved in the local campaign in Gorgie/Dalry, and was convinced that locally organised non-payment would be the most effective strategy, that Militant started to mobilise. This went against the official Militant position. Indeed, in Central Region, their official position was to back the Labour Party 'Stop It' campaign. In the end, Russell Taylor won the argument, and once Militant had decided to commit their organisation fully, they began to 'use their whole bureaucratic machinery to establish groups they could control right from the start' (Allan Armstrong, Chair, Lothian Federation APTUs, 3/5/91). This raised serious questions about organisation and democracy in the movement which are discussed in the next chapter. But despite taking until July 29th 1988 to outline their strategy in the *Militant* newspaper, they were the only part of the established labour movement who put forward a strategically coherent policy.

Over the next few months, Militant, Community Resistance and other advocates of resistance debated four main strategies:

- Non-registration: a call on local people to ignore the fines and refuse to comply with the register which the councils were compiling in order to administer the poll tax.
- Non-payment: the main plank of a resist-

ance strategy – a call on individuals to refuse to pay. People were not asked to do this in isolation, they were encouraged to organise in local groups and were reassured that they would be defended whenever the councils tried to recover the debts.

- Non-implementation: a call on local councils not to implement the tax. It was argued by some that they should lead the struggle by setting illegal budgets and if necessary they should resign en masse.

- Non-collection: a call on trade unionists not to collect the tax. This was particularly aimed at the local government union NALGO whose members would be administering the tax, and the civil servants union CPSA who would be dealing with rebates and benefits.

In November 1987, Community Resistance held a conference on the Poll Tax, at the Glasgow City Hall. This conference supported both non-payment and non-registration. But, when the role of the trade unions and Labour councils were assessed, people were not optimistic that either would actively support the campaign:

> Councillors who refuse to prosecute will be surcharged by the government so there is no point in trying to 'persuade' them. Is there anything to be gained by forcing statements in public from councillors saying they'll oppose, to show them up later? This would just give them the role of the leaders of the opposition, their capitulation (which is inevitable) would weaken other responses.
> We should appeal to council staff to obstruct offices, but this will probably be unsuccessful given the past record of union opposition.
> *Conference minutes, 14/11/87.*

In retrospect, this analysis proved shrewd, as many of the councillors who did pledge themselves to opposition later implemented the tax, and the unions did almost nothing.

Delegates also discussed how complementary direct action tactics could be used. Occupations would both gain publicity and provide a basis for negotiation; council meetings could be disrupted; local schemes and neighbourhoods could be made into no-go areas for the sheriff officers.

Discussion of the use of petitions was revealing. Many activists were strongly against:

> because petitions lead to people getting the impression that they have done their bit and the people collecting the signatures will do the rest.

Others felt that petitions could be used as an opportunity to talk to people and persuade them to join local groups, but they were not seen as an end in themselves.

Local organisation was stressed. The conference concluded that:

> Self-organisation in the schemes is better than staying city-centre based. Look at where things are most likely to start. Leaf-

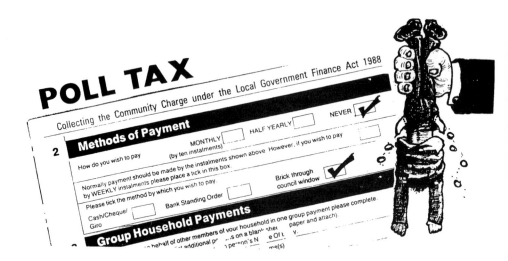

lets and posters should be seen as leading to the formation of local groups, then to public meetings.

To get the ball rolling we should either all concentrate on the areas we live in, or focus on areas where we have good contacts, and get these areas to act as a catalyst for others.

Conference minutes, 14/11/87.

The principles agreed at this conference were extremely important. They affirmed the embryonic strategy of the Maryhill Anti-Poll Tax Union, and confidently assessed the organisational needs of the future mass movement.

Militant followed suit in December 1987 when they set up an organisation called 'Labour Movement Against The Poll Tax' and, along with other Labour Left activists, they too called a strategy meeting in the Leith Town Hall. This meeting also discussed the four key strategic proposals of non-payment, non-implementation, non-collection and non-registration. Non-payment remained relatively uncontroversial and was accepted by virtually everyone at the conference, but important debates ensued over the issues of non-registration and non-collection.

The Revolutionary Democratic Group argued in favour of non-registration, suggesting that while it would not actually stop the tax, it would give confidence to the movement and would give it something concrete to organise around in the period before the Poll Tax was introduced. Militant argued that mounting a major non-registration campaign involved huge risks because, if the campaign failed, people would become disheartened. This, they thought, would prejudice the non-payment campaign. They also argued that there was no point in exposing people to huge fines for non-registration if this was not going to bring down the tax. Underlying the Militant perspective was their link to the Labour Party. Because one of their prime objectives was still to elect a Labour government, Militant supporters strongly resisted a campaign which would in-

WARNING

BAILIFFS BEWARE

POLL TAX FREE ZONE
ENTER AT YOUR OWN RISK

volve people in losing their vote because they were not on the electoral register. Community Resistance activists were split on the issue. In the end, the conference decided to support non-registration and as a result, many local groups took actions against the Poll Tax 'snoopers' (who were employed to compile the registers) but a full-scale campaign against registration was not mounted.

The other key debate at this conference was about the viability of a non-collection strategy and the role of the trade unions. Both Community Resistance and Militant were prepared to support a combined campaign of non-payment, non-implementation and non-collection (although Militants' emphasis was much more on non-payment). Others, primarily The Socialist Workers Party, argued that:

Many said that the real community charge was the resistance of the community.

> Community organisation stands in stark contrast to the power of workers organised in the work-place. Community politics diverts people away from the means to win, from the need to mobilise working class activity on a collective basis. And by putting the emphasis on the individuals will to resist, difficulties and defeats will be the

Rob Houn

responsibility of the individual alone...
    The biggest danger for socialists is to
ignore this dereliction of duty and substitute individual non-payment organised
through community campaigns for mass
working class action.
Socialist Workers Party pamphlet, 1988.

The Socialist Workers Party didn't believe that
the community had the political and economic
muscle to tackle the government. They thought
that because the working class had struggled
through a difficult period in the '80s, it would
be impossible to confront the state through
extra-parliamentary activity. This perspective
led them to stress requests for both Labour and
Trade Union leaders to act on behalf of the
working class - fortunately it was not widely
shared within the movement as a whole.

    Both of these early conferences stressed the
importance of local organisation in the tradition of the Maryhill Anti-Poll Tax Union and,
from the end of 1987 both set out to form local
Anti-Poll Tax Unions throughout Scotland.
The two political ideologies which underlay
the Community Resistance networks and the
Militant Tendency, became the dominant
ideological strands in the movement. Militant
was particularly influential in Dundee and
Glasgow. Non-aligned groups (inspired by
Community Resistance) were strongest in
Central Region, Aberdeen, the highlands and
the borders. Edinburgh had a fairly mixed influence throughout the campaign.

    In January 1988, most of the existing Edin-
burgh groups began to network together,
meeting regularly in the Edinburgh Unemployed Workers' Centre. The various Anti-Poll
Tax Unions, Community Resistance groups
and other Anti-Poll Tax organisations agreed
to form the Edinburgh Federation of Anti-Poll
Tax groups – the first city-wide federation in
the UK.

    From this point the non-payment cam-
paign began to build, and local groups were
formed throughout the whole of Edinburgh
and Glasgow. By July 1988, Strathclyde had

also formed a federation. Its founding conference was attended by 330 delegates from 96 organisations. By April 1989, when the Poll Tax was implemented, Glasgow had over 50 local Anti-Poll Tax Unions and Edinburgh over 40.

But, the growth of this community-based Anti-Poll Tax movement didn't go unchallenged by Labour politicians. In January 1988, Neil Kinnock addressed the Scottish local government conference, in Edinburgh. He denounced non-payment as 'fruitless' and 'a policy of despair'. He suggested that to adopt such a policy would be to enter 'a sort of dreamland' (*The Guardian*, 30/1/88). At this conference Kinnock tried to boost the 'Stop It' campaign, by calling a press conference at which he became the first signatory to a national petition against the Poll Tax. The petition read:

> We the undersigned believe that the Poll Tax is a fundamentally immoral tax, that it is unjust and unfair, that it will generally discriminate against those least able to pay, that the government must change its mind and the Poll Tax should be abandoned.

That the government must change its mind! – Who was living in dreamland?

The Scottish Trade Union Congress (STUC) decided it too had better do something.

> 'People like Campbell Christie (the STUC General Secretary) could see that things were happening from below and decided that they needed to pre-empt it.
> *Allan Armstrong, Chair, Lothian Federation APTUs.*

He was acutely embarrassed to learn that there was already a 'Stop It' campaign in existence. On January 6th, he admitted 'I wasn't aware of what stage 'Stop It' was in their campaign' (Labour, the Assembly and the Poll Tax, 1988). This major Labour Party campaign which was supposed to be leading the opposition to the Poll Tax had apparently gone unnoticed by the Secretary of the Scottish TUC- not a great testimony to its impact. Until the March 1988 Labour Conference, no 'Stop It' action had actually taken place. After the conference the STUC took over the campaign and attempted to put some life into it. According to a Labour Briefing pamphlet of the time, one conference observer commented that:

> The STUC had brought more drive and ideas in an afternoon than 'Stop It' in a year. Those who have experienced STUC campaigns may find this statement surprising, but it appears to be warranted.

In April, Campbell Christie tried to set up an umbrella campaign which would include dissident Tories, church groups, the SNP and everyone else. The SNP refused to join because the STUC was not prepared to support any form of non-payment campaign, and days before the new 'Stop It' campaign was due to be launched, the Scottish National party (SNP) stole the initiative. The SNP national executive endorsed a position of support for a non-pay-

The Poll Tax
If you think it's wrong, sign here.

Labour is leading a national Protest against Poll Tax.

We're protesting because it's unfair. An elderly widow in a flat will pay the same as a rich man in a mansion.

We're protesting because most of us will be paying far more for council services.

We're protesting because it allows an army of poll tax officers to demand personal information; because it takes decisions away from the councillors we elect and gives them to Government Ministers; because Poll Tax will cost over twice as much to collect as rates.

Our Poll Tax Protest will tell the Government they're wrong. It will bring home to them the resentment

and anger that this measure causes.

This is your chance to register your protest against Poll Tax. Your name can make the difference. When you join with the many that have already declared themselves, you make sure that a concerted cry of protest is heard throughout Britain.

If you'd like to be included, or want further information, sign your name. Fill out your details and send the whole advertisement to the address below. We'll add your name to our campaign.

Labour says that tax should be fair and based on ability to pay.

Poll Tax is an outrage. Join us in fighting it.

Labour

| Your signature | X |

YES I think the Poll Tax is undemocratic, unjust and fundamentally wrong. Please add my name to Labour's National Protest.

Full Name (BLOCK & CAPITALS PLEASE) _____ Address _____

Postcode _____ PT1

Please accept my donation of (please tick) £50 □ £25 □ £10 □ Other £_____ to help with the Poll Tax Protest (please make cheques/postal orders payable to the Labour Party).

□ (Please tick) I would like to join the Labour Party, please send me details. Return this entire advert to The Labour Party, Room 313, FREEPOST, London SE17 1BR. Thank you.

The Poll Tax
PROTEST

The Labour Party seemed to think that if it got enough people to sign the petition they would get rid of the Poll Tax.

ment campaign. They dismissed Labour's non-registration platform as a 'failed campaign'. The SNP's policy vice-chair Kenny MacAskill stated 'We now have the moral obligation to lead the non-payment, Anti-Poll Tax movement' (*Glasgow Herald* 16/5/88).

The Scottish National Party resented the imposition of regressive English laws on their country and used Scottish Nationalism as a powerful driving force for their campaign. The growing resentment of the Scottish people had been demonstrated by the General Election results, when the Tories had lost another eleven parliamentary seats in Scotland, and were reduced to just ten MPs. The SNP linked the fight against the Poll Tax to the fight for independence which they argued justified a call for civil disobedience.

Their approach was based on a long tradition of protest-oriented civil disobedience. This approach can be exemplified by the campaigns mounted by the peace movement in the early '80s. Then thousands of activists climbed into military bases; sat on runways; explored bunkers; some damaged military equipment. Most activists involved didn't expect that militarisation would end as a direct result of their actions or that they could physically prevent Cruise missiles from operating. What they wanted was to influence public opinion; to make arms control an electoral issue; to force the Labour Party into commitments, such as abandoning Cruise and Trident missiles. Civil disobedience was a way of expressing personal moral dissent. The individual was able to say 'you may go ahead with this policy, but not in my name, I will not co-operate'. This was the underlying position of the SNP in relation to the Poll Tax. So they called for 100,000 people who could afford to pay the tax, but were morally opposed to it, to pledge themselves to non-payment:

> If 100,000 Scots are prepared to say no to paying the Poll Tax, that is going to put unbearable pressure on the Tory's position in Scotland. Our judgement is that would

be enough to make the government back down.
Kenny MacAskill, Vice Chair, SNP, Scotsman, 12/1/88.

Although their tactics were more radical than Labour's, their strategic aim was similar to 'Stop It' in that it was geared towards changing the government's mind – civil disobedience used as a form of protest. Indeed, this largely middle class protest was dubbed the 'Can Pay, Won't Pay' campaign, to contrast it with the APTUs 'Can't Pay, Won't Pay' campaign.

The major problem with the SNP campaign was that its work was focused largely within its own ranks and, while many of its members were involved in the local Anti-Poll Tax Unions, as a national organisation its major role became to legitimise non-payment, not to organise it. Nevertheless, it did contribute towards a ground-swell of acceptance for the strategy.

The launch of the SNP campaign was a setback for the Labour Party and STUC, who could see that they were being undercut. But the STUC decided to push ahead with its own proposals anyway. Its 'six point plan' included:

- Sending Poll Tax forms back.
- The disruption of parliament.
- Mass appeals against having names put on the register.
- Pressure on local authorities to give the new tax only minimum support.
- Two massive public rallies – possibly this June and October.
- A major non-payment campaign if there is public support for such a move.
Glasgow Evening Times, 5/5/88.

By this time Campbell Christie was unable to dismiss non-payment completely. In launching the STUC campaign he was forced to sit on the fence:

This tax will have a drastic effect on people throughout Scotland and drastic action is needed. We will press ahead with a non-payment campaign, but only if there is a mandate from the public.

This was a scenario that the Labour Party desperately wanted to head off. But the pressure for non-payment was growing. A Mori poll published in *The Scotsman* (11/3/88) had indicated that 42% of the Scottish population were prepared to support a non-payment campaign and the new Anti-Poll Tax Unions were beginning to exercise a powerful influence. At the Scottish Labour Party Conference in Perth the month before, heavy lobbying from the Anti-Poll Tax Unions led to a decision to postpone the debate on the Poll Tax until September. The Labour establishment feared that they might end up committed to a campaign of non-payment, if a vote were taken at that meeting. They were particularly worried about the

effect on their own supporters of the near doubling of the SNP vote from 11.1% in 1984 to 21% in the district elections on May 12th.

But Kinnock had made it clear in January that the Labour Party would not get embroiled in 'an illegal campaign' and as far as the leadership was concerned, that position was not negotiable. This was demonstrated by the way in which Robin Cook, Labour's Shadow Health Secretary (a prominent supporter of non-payment), was 'silenced' by the party. An agreement was hammered out, in which he 'agreed not to make any further comments encouraging non-payment or to discuss this with the press. But in return it was agreed, albeit reluctantly by some of those present, he himself would not have to pay it' (*The Scotsman*, 19/8/88).

In September, the STUC called a week of action against the Poll Tax, the centre piece of which was an eleven-minute stoppage on the 13th, during which the Scottish people 'were asked to demonstrate their anger by stopping what they were doing to sign petitions, sound car horns, ring church bells and join local campaign initiatives' (*The Scotsman*, 19/8/91). They printed 500,000 window bills and mailed material to 3,500 organisations. The STUC said it would escalate its campaign against the Poll Tax if this event was successful. But it was difficult for anyone to take an eleven-minute stoppage seriously, and the lack of response enabled delegates at the special Labour Party conference on the Poll Tax in Govan to argue that this indicated there was no support for non-payment.

The conference, held on September 17th, endorsed the Labour National Executive position by a two to one majority. The *Evening Mail* reported (18/9/88):

> The majority of delegates in the hall seemed to support non-payment, but the vote was carried by the block vote of the big unions and the constituencies.

This signalled both the conservative role that the trade unions were to play and highlighted the distinction between the leaders and officials of the Labour Party, and many ordinary Labour Party members who backed non-payment throughout the campaign.

Following the substantial defeat of a non-payment position at the Govan conference, a number of 'dissident' MPs decided to set up a Committee of 100. This was to be made up of 'prominent Scots' who would refuse to pay the Poll Tax. The main movers of this campaign were the MPs Dick Douglas, John McAllion, and Maria Fyfe. At the press conference, on the 23rd of September, Dick Douglas defended his position:

> I know what it is like not to eat. I watched my mother grow old before her time, worrying about where her family's next meal was coming from. I was born into a life of extreme poverty in Govan. I joined the Labour Party because its main aim is to protect people who are in difficult circumstances. I'm compelled, because of my background, to take this particular stance: not to pay the Poll Tax. The Poll Tax is the most vexatious and class-ridden piece of legislation I have ever seen. There will be many who cannot pay it. The only way I can demonstrate to my constituents that there is no shame in not being able to pay this tax is to stand beside them.

He saw the launch of the Committee of 100 as the first step in a campaign in which they would build:

> a kind of pyramid structure with local groupings of prominent non-payers located in different parts of the country.
> *The Glasgow Herald, 19/9/88.*

AH
HUVNAE
RYED

It was a non-party political campaign and got qualified support from the SNP: 'A committee of 100 is not as ambitious as our army of 100,000 non-payers, but... we would welcome anyone moving towards the non-payment position, whether it is 100 Scottish big-wigs or whatever.' The committees never really got off the ground because they had no strategic direction but, like the SNP initiative, they added legitimacy to the campaign of non-payment and indirectly helped to build the local Anti-Poll Tax Unions.

On November 10th 1988, the Govan by-election further rocked the Labour establishment. Jim Sillars, an SNP vice-president who campaigned on a platform of non-payment, overturned a Labour majority of 19,509 to win by 2,500 votes. It was clear to all but the Labour Party that they lost because they had done nothing to oppose the Poll Tax. By this time their campaign had run into the ground. They hadn't organised a single demonstration against the tax and most Labour councils were already committed to collecting it.

On April 1st 1989, when the Poll Tax was implemented in Scotland, the STUC did manage to organise an official protest march in Edinburgh. This was attended by 30,000 people, but it was only this big because of a mass-mobilisation by the Anti-Poll Tax Unions. Once the Poll Tax was implemented, the protest campaign had nowhere to go. In November the STUC held a miserable demonstration in Glasgow for which there was virtually no official organisation. It ended up in a car park with no sound system for the speakers. This was their last significant gesture of opposition to the tax.

Can't Pay, Won't Pay

As the protest campaign diminished, the resistance campaign grew. By March 1989 over 15,000 non-payers had marched in Glasgow under the banner of the Anti-Poll Tax Federation and support for non-payment was mushrooming. Labour policy-makers had failed to grasp that for most people non-payment came from the harsh reality of their economic experience, not a theoretical commitment to resistance. The arguments were overwhelming.

1381:

The Peasants

Revolt

The so called 'Community Charge' was not dubbed the Poll Tax for nothing. It was named after a head tax imposed on the people of Britain in 1381. The parallels are striking. In order to pay for war, the Lords and the Gentry imposed a Poll Tax on every man and woman over the age of 15. Suddenly the population of England appeared to drop by a third as people refused to pay, or dropped off the register. The tax was resented everywhere and was widely evaded. Commissioners with armed escorts were set around the country to collect the arrears but they were disarmed and chased away. After a second and more determined attempt to collect the tax, uprisings broke out throughout England. Building from Essex and Kent the rebellion spread to London under the leadership of Wat Tyler and Thomas Faringdon. The Chancellor, and Archbichop were executed by the peasants on Tower Hill. The King was confronted at Smithfield where Wat Tyler was killed. To appease the rebels the King agreed to their de-

People couldn't afford to pay. Many were living well below the poverty line and had no room to manoeuvre. Paying the Poll Tax would mean not paying something else. This would result in increased rent arrears; mortgage defaults; electricity and telephones cut off; or borrowing from the loan sharks. The choice for many was whether to eat and clothe their children properly or pay the tax.

Given this, strong moral pressure was placed on those who could afford to pay to stand with those who could not. Activists argued that it was not tenable for those who were secure to protest against the Poll Tax while others with no choice but to resist, faced poindings and warrant sales (and in England and Wales the prospect of being dragged through the courts and threatened with imprisonment).

Waiting for the Labour Party to win the next election was not an option. Nobody could guarantee that they would win and people couldn't afford to wait three or four years. They would be facing bailiffs or sheriff officers within months. Even if the Labour Party did get elected, they seemed in no hurry to abolish the tax. Official Labour Party policy stated that it would take at least two years to abolish (and that was after the general election). Martin Luther King once wrote:

> For years now I have heard the word 'wait'. It rings in the ear of every negro with piercing familiarity. The 'wait' has almost always meant never.
>
> *Martin Luther King, Why We Can Never Wait, 1964.*

Many people saw similarities, and having witnessed the half hearted 'Stop It' campaign, some didn't believe that the Poll Tax would be abolished even if the Labour Party came to power.

The arguments in favour of non-payment were also forged out of the bitter experiences of the '80s. The miners had been heavily defeated in 1985 and many thought that if *they* couldn't defeat the government then no one could. It was clear, from a very early stage, that the trade unions would not be prepared to lead a campaign against the Poll Tax. Likewise, many local councillors who had watched Liverpool and Lambeth councillors fined and disqualified from office in their attempted to resist rate capping, were reluctant to get involved. It was obvious that it would be a waste of time petitioning central government. The GLC had the support of more than 80% of Londoners, but it was still happily abolished by the Tories. The ambulance workers produced a petition of over 6 million signatures – the biggest petition ever – and this was totally ignored. So, the campaign had to be led by the community and non-payment was a strategy which couldn't be ignored because the government had to recover the money.

The precedents for civil disobedience were strong and examples were cited in all the early Anti-Poll Tax meetings. Women would not have the vote if the suffragettes hadn't broken the law. Trade Unions would not have gained the right to strike. In Eastern Europe many would still be under totalitarian rule if they hadn't broken the law. America, the so-called bastion of democracy, fought for its independence under the slogan: 'no taxation without representation'. There were also *direct* precedents for resistance of this kind. In Scotland the Glasgow rent strikes of 1915 were an important inspiration and in England the story of the peasants revolt against the Poll Tax in 1831 was told in virtually every meeting.

Calling on these traditions was an important part of explaining why non-co-operation was needed, so too was the use of the strike as an analogy. People generally accept that if an employer imposes working conditions which are collectively unacceptable, then the workforce has a right to withdraw its labour. Even after Thatcher's union reforms the right to strike is still accepted as an important democratic principle, where the majority of the work-force is in favour. The imposition of the Poll Tax seemed similar. The vast majority of people considered the Poll Tax unacceptable

mands, but anger against the death of Wat Tyler sparked rebellion once again. The risings spread throughout the South West. There were riots in Bridgwater, Winchester, Salisbury, Hertfordshire and Cambridgeshire. The revolt spread as far North as Yorkshire and Cheshire. The King reneged on his promises and hunted down the ringleaders. Nevertheless, most people were granted an amnesty, and it was a long time before any government tried to introduce such a regressive tax on the people again.

The 1915 Glasgow Rent Strikes

In 1915 rent rises were announced throughout the City of Glasgow. Very soon over 15,000 tenants had refused to pay. Collectors were harassed and were forced to abandon their attempts to collect the money. When eighteen munitions workers were summoned to court, thousands of Glasgow women took to the streets. A general strike was called for November 22nd, but the government backed down and reduced rents to the prewar level.

49

and consequently believed they had the right to withdraw their co-operation.

Unlike the rich (who use creative accountants to avoid paying taxes) and large corporate companies (who owe billions to the treasury), most of the people who joined the non-payment campaign were 'honest, law abiding citizens' who had never broken the law before. For them, the Poll Tax was the last straw – an exceptional imposition on their lives which had to be dealt with by exceptional means. Because of this, virtually everyone who actively opposed the Poll Tax came behind the strategy of non-payment. As Allan Armstrong (Lothian Federation Chair) said:

Saying no to the Poll Tax 1381

Everyone was in complete opposition to the 'Stop It' campaign which was seen as a complete waste of time, so non-payment was never an issue.

This is verified by my own experience in the South West of England. In February and March 1990, just before the Poll Tax was implemented in England and Wales, Robin Clapp (Press Officer of the Avon Federation of Anti-Poll Tax Unions) and I (Secretary) spoke at over 80 public meetings, organised in local community centres and work-places. Most of these meetings were attended by well over 50 people, some by over 200. Often strategy was discussed for the first time at these meetings. Yet, after we had put the arguments and asked at the end of each meeting how many people would be paying, only two or three said that they would. Some must have shifted a long way to get to this position:

'I've been a Conservative voter since the time of Macmillan, but I'm proud to stand up at this meeting and say that I will refuse to pay this tax!' This pledge from a local publican met warm applause at a 40 strong Anti-Poll Tax meeting in Ilchester. He went on to offer free use of a pub room with tea and coffee laid on for future meetings of the non-payment campaign.
Somerset Clarion, May 1990.

Despite this, the Labour Party continued to oppose the campaign. By the end of 1988, with no credible campaign of their own they were indistinguishable from the Tories in their attacks on non-payers. But non-payment continued to grow. By April 1990, official figures for Scotland showed that nearly a million people hadn't paid a penny, and tens of thousands of people were organised into local Anti-Poll Tax Unions.

3

THE ANTI-POLL TAX
UNIONS

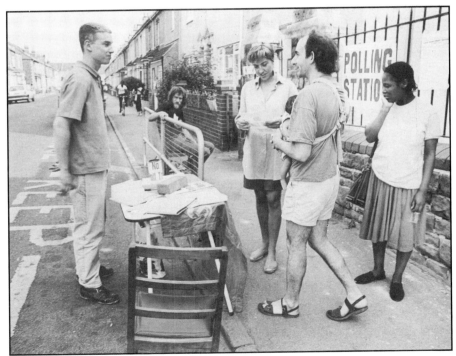

Mark Simmons

Organising In The Neighbourhoods

I had taken the decision that I wasn't going to pay, but it got to November 1989 and I thought hell! Where's the support that we're supposed to get from the SNP? We heard a lot about the One Hundred Campaign, but they didn't come into the villages and towns of Midlothian. So we were starting to get a bit worried. There were a few women kept phoning me and saying 'Are you still not paying?' 'No, I'm not paying,' I said, 'We should get together. I've heard of a group in Edinburgh, Prestonfield – I work near there, why don't we go along one night?' So my sister, myself, one of her friends, and my daughter went along to Prestonfield. We just sat and listened. We were amazed... Look at all these people that know what they're doing! Every one of them was so confident. We left Prestonfield that night with a donation of money from them to start our own group, and a promise from them that if we had our first public meeting they'd send somebody out to help us. So I phoned round people that I knew... To save time, we decided to have the meeting in the house, so there must have been about a dozen people turned up and Kenny Curtis, from Prestonfield he came out and advised us on how to start up our group. We held our first public meeting a couple of weeks after that and we got 60 people.

Chris Moyers, Mayfield APTU, Midlothian, 6/5/91.

YOU TOLD ME BEN NEVIS WAS THE HIGHEST MOUNTAIN IN SCOTLAND!

By the end of 1988, the majority of city neighbourhoods, most towns and many villages in Scotland had an Anti-Poll Tax Union (APTU). In England and Wales there was a buzz of excitement as information trickled out about the growing non-payment campaign. Commu-

nity Resistance produced an information pack and sent literally hundreds to contacts across the border. Speakers went to Sheffield, London, Leeds, Norwich, South Wales and many other cities. Some of these areas twinned with Prestonfield and other Scottish neighbourhoods (an idea taken from the miners' strike) and, by the end of 1988, local groups started forming in England and Wales. By November 1989, there were over 1,000 local Anti-Poll Tax Unions in Britain. These were the organisations from which the real assault on the Poll Tax was launched.

The groups which formed were small at first, often with only five of six activists but within months many unions had built up memberships of over 200 people. Some had signed up over 500. Typically, the Anti-Poll Tax Unions covered small areas about the size of a political ward. They operated in the heart of the community. Meetings were held at first in people's homes, and then in pubs, community centres and local halls:

> 30 people were crammed into the living-room which can't have been more than ten-foot square. People were sitting on the arms of the chairs and on the floor, there wasn't even room to open and shut the door, but everyone got a cup of tea and

time was allowed for everyone to explain
who they were and where they lived.
Danny Burns, extract from diary, May 1989.

People talked openly about their personal
hardship and, while non-payment became the
dominant political strategy for the campaign,
in most APTUs everyone was welcome to the
local group, whether they were non-payers or
not. Many groups started like the Mayfield
group described above. They were built on
personal networks – people who knew people,
who knew other people. Sometimes these over-
lapped with the mainstream political networks, often they didn't.

Activity in most areas started with public
meetings. In Bristol alone well over 100 meetings were held between February and May
1989. The numbers attending these first meetings were huge.

I spoke to a local meeting of over 500 people
in Bridgwater. In Plymouth a crowd of 200
stood in the street as I arrived to speak and 200
more were inside. The Hall only held
200 people, so we had to have two meetings,
and those outside waited for an hour and a half
until the first meeting had ended. I attended
many meetings in small outlying areas whose
councils were mostly Tory controlled. One was
the village of Cromhall in North Avon. Out of
a population of around 500 over 120 turned up
to the meeting and 40 stayed behind to discuss
the formation of an Anti-Poll Tax Union. In
other areas the meetings were even bigger. The
Anti-Poll Tax Union in Haringey organised a
borough wide meeting with Tony Benn as a
speaker and over 1,000 people turned up. People were hungry for information:

They organised within that year to make
sure that every single town and village
around Morley had a meeting. Me and a
young student Jo went along to a meeting
which had been organised in East Ardsley
which is a large village on the edge of
Morley. It was held in the local community
centre. They only had room for about 100

or so people but 250 crowded in. When we
turned up at this place there wasn't a single
light on in the village, the whole community had come to that meeting. Jo had
never spoken at a meeting anything like
that before, she felt nervous and quite
humbled that all these people should be
hanging on her every word.
Ian Greaves, Secretary, Leeds Federation APTUs, 11/5/91.

Some groups used theatre and entertainment as a way of spreading information. The
Aberdeen Anti-Poll Tax group was formed
when people from the radical bookshop came
together with a community arts group:

More and more people kept coming in and
asking what was being done about the Poll
Tax... The local community arts group had
a theatre group called 'Wise Up' and they
got a show together about the Poll Tax.
They took this show around the estates
with information for people about registration and how to fight it, to encourage them
to set up local groups and support networks. The plays were performed in local
community centres. Attendance for the
plays varied from about 10 to 40 or more.
The meetings which followed were encouraging because people gave their names as
contacts or asked people to set up future
meetings.
Charles Wood, Aberdeen APTU, 16/4/91.

The public meetings formed the embryo of the
new groups, and each group as it was set up
helped others to start:

We started our group. We put out our
phone number and we started getting calls
from all over. It was far too much for us to
handle. Midlothian is a very big area, so we
decided that we had to set up groups in
other areas, so we did a Prestonfield.
They'd helped us, so we went out and
helped other groups... just by getting in
touch with people in the area, people that

we knew, and said 'why don't you start a group and we'll come and help you start it?' So we started one in Dalkeith, we gave them advice. We also gave them a donation, and then we started one in Gorebridge... this is all areas in Midlothian. We started Pathhead, Penicuik, Bonnyrigg and, as a result of going down to Dunbar on the same day as a poinding, we managed to set up a group in Dunbar. So that was Midlothian pretty well-covered. We felt quite proud of ourselves that we'd gone out and made other groups start themselves.

Chris Moyers, Mayfield APTU, Midlothian, 6/5/91.

People from every conceivable background came to Anti-Poll Tax meetings.

In my local group, Easton in Bristol (a residential neighbourhood of small terraces with very few public shopping streets) the union was built up through a door-to-door campaign. A group of five or six people (mostly friends) formed the core. They advertised a public meeting on the Poll Tax and about 50 people turned up. Out of these some joined the organising group. This small group then mass-produced a window poster which said 'No Poll

Mark Simmons

58

Tax Here'. The poster was dropped through the letter-boxes of 2000 households and the group waited to see who put them up. Posters appeared in about 100 windows. Activists then went round and spoke to these people individually, inviting them to attend the next organising meeting, about fifteen did – enough to form the core of a group.

At the next meeting the whole neighbourhood was divided into areas of three or four streets and each group member was given responsibility for an area. This meant leafletting regularly, acting as the local contact and advice point, and also identifying further activists in their 'patch'. The aim was to get down to street level organisation. There was an incentive for the area representatives to do this because the more people they got involved, the less responsibility they had to take on themselves.

This network was strengthened by a door-to-door survey of over 500 households. The survey was not intended to be scientifically accurate. Its purpose was to give the APTU a fairly accurate picture of what was happening on the ground, and, perhaps more signifi-

Hanging on every word -

local people were hungry

for information.

Mark Simmons

cantly, it was a pretext for engaging people in conversation about the Poll Tax, informing them of the non-payment campaign and encouraging them to join their local APTU. The results were interesting. Only 20% said that they would definitely pay. The same number said that they would definitely not, but most significantly, 55% said that they wouldn't pay if a lot of other people in the area weren't paying either. So even at this early stage we knew that non-payment was going to be massive. Over a third of the people canvassed became paid up members of the union. By the end of the exercise Easton had over 300 members and street reps for almost every street.

The canvass was not left there. The key to its success was the second visit. The group compiled all the statistics on a street by street basis and many of the reps then went back, door-to-door, and told people the results of the survey in their street and the neighbouring streets. A newsletter was delivered to everyone telling them what the overall results were for Easton. This meant that people knew how few of their neighbours were going to pay and it gave them confidence not to pay themselves. They had spoken to the canvassers personally, so they knew that the survey was genuine. Soon after, a public meeting was held in Easton which attracted 300 people. This steadily increasing growth was typical of the way many APTUs developed.

Much of the early work of the Anti-Poll Tax Unions was spent listening to information about people's personal financial circumstances. Often time was put aside at the beginning and end of each meeting to answer questions about individual problems. This was important because it gave newcomers a sense that people cared and that they were not just being talked at. They saw:

> It was ordinary people that were there. It was nobody that was going to sit at a top table with a dicky bow. It was one of their own.
>
> *Jackie Moyers, Mayfield APTU, Midlothian, 6/5/91.*

Mark Simmons

Many people were already up to their necks in debt and some had started cutting back on food and clothing. Often they couldn't see a way out of their difficulties, so giving them the confidence to consider collective action was vital:

> This was a wee housing estate built between the wars, and re-housed slum people from the south side of the city. So we've now got a population of very old people. It's a whole generation of people who remember warrant sales, who remember that you don't get in debt even if you do without food. We had quite a job on our hands... We had a woman in tears, quite hysterical at a meeting, just because she was at the end of her tether. She was already doing without food, already not having the heating on, and still trying to pay the rent, so where the hell was she going to find any other money?
>
> *Sadie Rooney, Prestonfield Community Resistance Against The Poll Tax, Edinburgh, 10/5/91.*

These discussions were particularly important because people felt isolated. Some people lived on their own, others received little support, and in some cases outright hostility, from their families. Another story from Prestonfield shows how, as in the miners' strike, families were split down the middle:

> We had one woman who had to hide her Poll Tax books from her husband. He pays and she hasn't paid. In fact it's a guessing game in the group. Where has Rosalind hid her Poll Tax books?! Because he's had the house upside down trying to find these books. Because if he found them he would go and pay it for her. But she's so determined that she won't pay, and that's caused a lot of hassle in their marriage, but she's stuck to her guns and not paid.
>
> *Sadie Rooney, Prestonfield Community Resistance, Edinburgh, 10/5/91.*

Focused personal contact helped to build a

Mark Simmons

Mark Simmons

feeling of solidarity, and this in turn supported the building of organisation at the most local level. The work of one street rep in my local group shows how important this was. An independent television company approached the Easton group in order to work with us on a film about the Poll Tax. The film was never shown, but the way the community was engaged in the process of making it is instructive. The film producers wanted a shot of all the doors in the street, opening one by one as the occupants came out of their houses with banners and signs. Charles, the local street rep, went round to people's houses every evening for a week and explained to them what was wanted. Out of 30 houses in the street (a cul-de-sac) 28 agreed to participate. The street is multi-racial with a fairly wide class mix. It was inspiring to see white working class men standing shoulder to shoulder with Asian women and their kids, holding the same banners and engrossed in conversation. Some of them had never spoken to each other before. The film was made, but more importantly, as result of making it, virtually every one of those households joined the Union, and most still had posters in their windows a year later. People were brought into the campaign, not through a leaflet or a canvasser, but through an interesting activity. They didn't have to go to the campaign, it came to them. It was this sort of localised work which created real trust and gave people the confidence to do things they would never have done before. In most areas, the focus was something other than a television programme; maybe a local 'bill burning' or the organisation of a street level public meeting.

Information and support was not only passed on through direct contact with the Anti-Poll Tax Unions. While these formed the backbone of the movements' organisation, an infinite number of informal networks were spreading information:

I think informal networks are important. It's difficult to quantify, but every so often I get a glimpse of that sort of thing. Like I was in

The burning of bills became a symbol of the movement. An act of defiance which took place in public demonstrations everywhere. Here people are enjoying themselves at a local event in St Werburghs, Bristol.

Stockbridge the other day and I ran into someone who was due to have a poinding a year ago, and was active in resisting that poinding but hasn't been involved in the group since. But I bumped into him in the street, and he'd heard that the sheriffs had been about, and he asked me for some leaflets. Obviously this was a topic of conversation in the pub, and so that was someone who I would no longer have considered as an activist but who was obviously still spreading information to their own friends and colleagues at work and so on. In a way it's like having a ripple effect. The activists who attend the meetings produce leaflets and put out leaflets. These get to people who are on the contact list but who maybe never go to a meeting, but I get the impression that these people themselves are considered advisers and experts by their own circle of friends. This goes on amongst work-mates and in the pub and all these sorts of informal circles.

Mike Vallance, Stockbridge Newtown APTU, Edinburgh, 6/5/91.

Many shops displayed information for the Anti-Poll Tax Unions.

Mark Simmons

Given that the campaign involved millions of people in refusing to pay the Poll Tax and only tens of thousands were involved as activists, the things people were talking about in the pubs and the chip shops probably had more influence than the local group meeting.

These informal networks were strengthened by the sheer visibility of the campaign at a local level. This was often the crucial factor in turning a local issue into a local talking point. This meant that the shops and shopping streets were also an important focus. In the Bedminster area of Bristol in the middle of 1989, the local group held a stall and engaged people through a petition on which the signatories stated their commitment to non-payment. On the first Saturday, 1,700 people signed it within three hours. The pavement was completely blocked; people were signing and then returning an hour later with their whole family. Similar scenes were repeated for the next four weeks.

In some areas you could walk down a whole shopping street and the majority of shops were displaying a 'Pay No Poll Tax' poster and information about the next local group meeting. In Bristol, the city council identified twenty newsagents who they hoped would collect the Poll Tax. Within weeks of the list being circulated six pulled out. Local communities made it plain that they would no longer use the shops if they continued to collect. In some cases they went further:

> Attacks and threats have been made against Bristol newsagents and shops where people can pay the Poll Tax. Windows have been smashed and graffiti daubed over businesses which have become agents for the Bristol-based company 'Penalty Points'. The firm installs special tills with its agents to collect the community charge on behalf of local authorities for a fee.
> Mr. Ross Hendry, a spokesman for the company... said 'because of the attacks, one newsagent in Patchway has now

declined taking an agency after a brick was thrown through his window.' He said another newsagent in Bishoport Avenue, Hartclife had the words 'Poll Tax scab' and 'you're the first' scrawled in white paint across his window. A Circle K store in Cardiff where the revolutionary scheme was launched on April 9th with 48 agents, had its door locks jammed with superglue.

Bristol Evening Post, 10/5/90.

While the council was still able to collect through local post offices, the newsagents' payment scheme proved a disaster.

Another reason the campaign had such a high profile was its saturation cover of information. The Strathclyde Federation of Anti-Poll Tax Unions produced over 250,000 copies of its first newsletter. The Leeds Federation produced over 100,000 of its first leaflet and, by mid-1990, the Haringey groups had delivered over a million leaflets door-to-door. Fly posting was an important part of this saturation approach, and was used to create an atmosphere of resistance. In many areas, every lamppost had an A5 notice stuck to it, telling people what to do if the bailiffs came round, and offering telephone numbers to ring if they needed advice or support. Housing schemes and estates were plastered with posters. One showing a vicious dog, read 'Bailiffs? Make my day!'. Another showing a picture of Malcolm X holding a machine gun looking out from behind the curtains, read: 'Bailiffs we're ready.' A third showed a picture of a bailiff swinging in a noose. It read 'Dead bailiffs don't knock on doors.' In some areas bailiffs and registration officers were photographed and their portraits were reproduced on posters which read 'wanted' and listed their 'crimes'. These images were extremely popular. They made people laugh, and because they were enjoyed they weren't ignored. People were used to seeing images of themselves in the role of victim. Now wherever they looked there were images of their adversaries in this role. This inspired confidence and a feeling of security. So when the local group declared their neighbourhood a bailiff-free zone, it didn't seem like the declaration of a distant committee. People could see it *was* a bailiff-free zone. Contrast this with the way in which traditional labour movement organisations handle information. A set of boring minutes once a year to the members and a totally uninspiring (but glossy) leaflet to the community at large once a year: 'What we are doing to help your community.' It is hard to imagine the local Labour Party executive committee endorsing a campaign to fly-post information onto every blank space; every lamppost; every street corner. It is even harder to imagine them actually doing it – wandering the streets with a plastic bag full of wallpaper paste concealing an old paint brush. The Labour Party represented conventional 'respectability'. This was the fundamental difference between them and the community who waged the campaign.

The posters which were fly-posted were only the tip of a massive iceberg of imagination. One of the great strengths of the movement was its diversity. While the central federation produced a number of standard leaflets, the local groups produced a myriad of different posters, leaflets, car stickers, etc. Over five groups in Bristol produced their own badges, as many produced their own Christmas cards. A great deal of imagination went into leaflets aimed at local work-forces. The Easton group in Bristol leafletted the local chocolate factory in an attempt to get them to set up a work-place Anti-Poll Tax Union. The Haringey group in London wrote a letter to post office workers asking them not to deliver Poll Tax notices. Activists posted these through all the pillar boxes – a very direct means of communication. On April 1st 1989, the Tottenham group held a theatrical street event – Mad Thatcher's Tea Party – at which they gave out tea-bags to celebrate 200 years since the Boston Tea Party (which began the revolt against another tax imposed by the British government). This diversity reinforced the image that local people had of a deep-

rooted movement in which many 'ordinary people' had become active. In most campaigns 'central office' produces thousands of leaflets which are then distributed locally. This can lead the general public to believe that there is no local campaign; that it is run by one person; or that it has no depth. In this campaign the local groups were not the passive arm of a centralised campaign but centres of energy and imagination.

Above: Hundreds of Christmas cards were produced by the campaign. This card showed the real impact of the Poll Tax. For many children it meant no Christmas at all.

Diversity also ensured that the campaign got extensive press coverage. In Bristol for most of the first year, there was something on the Poll Tax in virtually every edition of the *Evening Post*. Sometimes this related to decisions of the city council, but often it was a report of a creative action a local group had taken – a demonstration outside the Tory headquarters; or the burning of bills in local shopping streets; or, as in the case of Easton, a mock bailiff valuation at the house in which Tory MP Jonathan Sayeed was holding his surgery. In some areas, the police tried to stop the local meetings on the pretext that they posed a threat to public order. One meeting, due to be held in a pub in Nailsea, was cancelled as a result of police pressure on the landlord. The Anti-Poll

Tax Union were only expecting 30 or 40 people but, after the story of police intervention was splashed across the press, over 300 people turned up to a meeting in the car park of the same pub. Events and issues of press interest were reported under the names of the local group 'Montpelier APTU', 'Bedminster APTU' etc. Each had their own press contact, and if the press came through to the federation they would be referred to the local group. This dramatically multiplied the potential for press coverage.

Groups also got publicity by participating in local elections. In many areas, the polling booths were canvassed. In some, Anti-Poll Tax candidates took on the Labour establishment. In Scotland six independent Anti-Poll Tax activists, won between 21% and 34% of the vote, with Keith Simpson obtaining 1,682 votes in Musselborough (East Lothian). In Werneth (Oldham), the Anti-Poll Tax candidate polled 528 votes to Labour's 1,408 in the 1991 local council elections. More successful were the local Labour Party wards which stood non-payment candidates. In Bristol with every election, the size of the 'rebel' group of Labour councillors grew as more and more non-payment councillors were elected.

Within the movement there was some debate about whether this was an appropriate strategy. Militant opposed standing anyone against the Labour Party because they were 'the official party of the working class', even when Labour Party candidates were openly opposed to non-payment. This reached farcical proportions when they refused to campaign for one of their own supporters, Keith Simpson (a local councillor who had been thrown out of the Labour group because of his views on the Poll Tax), when he tried to get re-elected.

Other activists were opposed to an election campaign because they thought it would only legitimise the council, and that any elected councillor would be unable to change anything once elected anyway. But, despite these objections, many activists saw the elections as another way of raising the political profile of the

Mark Simmons

69

Anti-Poll Tax campaign, and a lot of very lively campaigns were run.

As the number of Anti-Poll Tax Unions grew, city and regional federations were formed to co-ordinate activities. The Avon Federation of APTUs met every three weeks for over two and a half years. Most meetings were attended by more than 70 delegates. Other city-wide federations were just as big. The role of these federations was to produce information economically; to co-ordinate advice and information through the office, and to organise city-wide events from fundraising benefit gigs to demonstrations, council lobbies and occupations. Most federations organised big bill burning demonstrations when the Poll Tax was being set.

Some of these events were interesting because of the way that they combined local organisation with a central focus. Following the implementation of the Poll Tax in April 1990, both Leeds and Bristol organised 'Star Marches'. These involved people marching into the centre of the city from various local neighbourhoods. Because they had a local focus, they were able to reach out to working class areas. The local meeting point was not just an assembly point. Local people were leafletted by the local APTU and asked to gather on a local green to burn their bills. Speeches and music were organised for each small locality. A brazier for burning was located on each green. This meant that older people or parents with children, who couldn't easily walk into the centre, were able to attend a local event, while other people who thought they wouldn't go to the centre, did so when they met all their friends at the local event.

Some of the city-wide federations set up campaign offices. Offices were opened in Glasgow, London, Leeds and Bristol. These were staffed full-time by volunteers and became an important central focus for the campaign. By ringing the office, people were able to get personal advice and were put in contact with the Anti-Poll Tax Union in their local area. Distribution of coach tickets to demonstrations was

organised there; leaflets and posters were
stocked there, they also acted as a co-ordination point for the local groups. In Bristol when
the court cases started (see Chapter 5), each
person with a summons, who rang into the
office, was logged and sent an information
pack. The same personal attention was given to
people with notices from the bailiffs. At the
peak of the campaign, the Bristol office was
staffed morning and afternoon five days a
week by different volunteers. Between February and May 1990, it was receiving over 200
calls a week. Large numbers of volunteers were
co-ordinated through the offices. In Bristol, in
addition to the eight functional officers, there
were up to fifteen volunteer office workers

Mark Simmons

Federations produced and

distributed leaflets and

posters in large quantities.

Bristol Evening Post

Danny Burns working in the office of the Avon Federation of Anti Poll Tax Unions.

(although this number dwindled by late 1990), at least five court support workers and two people specialising in bailiff monitoring. Most of these activists did at least a day's work for the city-wide federation, in addition to the work they were doing for their local groups. Raising money and monitoring also took time. The Bristol campaign alone had a turnover of over £20,000. Benefit gigs and jumble sales were organised and raised vast sums of money. The St. Werburgh's group in Bristol raised £500 on one night. The Easton group raised £650 with a day of jumble sales and videos, and an evening of entertainment. The Leeds Federation raised £3,000 for the campaign when 'The Wedding Present', a local band, held a benefit gig.

These activities probably involved more people in local organisation than any other campaign in British history. Local Anti-Poll Tax Unions engaged people who had never been involved in organised politics before. Lo-

Tommy Sheridan and Jeanette McGuin outside the office of the Strathclyde Federation of Anti-Poll Tax Unions.

cal organisation was the key to success because it enabled groups to tap into informal networks. These sustained the vast levels of non-payment, which in turn sustained the campaign through the lulls in political activity.

Democracy In The Movement

Despite these achievements not all groups operated in such a dynamic and open way. There was a big difference between those which were run by independent activists and many others (albeit the minority) which were dominated or controlled by political groups.

Most non-aligned groups found it necessary to have a minimum of clearly identifiable 'officers' (such as a secretary and treasurer), but these people were elected to do a job, not to exercise executive power. The atmosphere of these groups tended to be extremely informal, and this made it possible to involve people who were not used to public meetings and keep them interested:

We had our first proper public meeting and we went through all of the rigmarole of electing a chair, a treasurer and a secretary and things like that, making it official. We had one member who was very officious and wanted everything done right. We couldn't quite see the point. We just wanted to get out there and fight against sheriff officers.
Chris Moyers, Mayfield APTU, Midlothian, 6/5/91,

We rotate the chair at every meeting. People take the chair now who would never have dreamed of taking chairs of anything. That's the beauty of it. It's great. It's become a social education.
Linda Wright, Prestonfield Community Resistance, 10/5/91.

Often groups sent delegates to federation meetings on a rotation basis in order to encourage as many people as possible to become involved in the city and regional co-ordination.

Many of the groups set up by Militant operated in a different way. Militant would call public meetings (which were often well attended) and then, often at the same meetings, call for elections to determine who would make up the executive committee and who would be delegated to the federation. Whereas most members of the public had very little free time, many of the Militant members were either unemployed and had time on their hands, or lived 'the political life', going to meetings every evening. Most ordinary people at those meetings didn't know each other and had little political experience, so they voted for the people who had set up the meeting. As a result, large numbers of delegates to regional and city federations were Militant supporters – often the only ones in their group, and as such extremely unrepresentative.

In these local groups, the executive became a decision-making body which on election went away and did the work of the Anti-Poll Tax Union. Public meetings would be advertised now and again, but the public were not involved in the general running of the union. This had a damaging effect on the level of public activity in those areas because the campaign was unable to make effective contact with the all important informal networks. It also meant that those who had been elected were totally unaccountable to their groups. Militant members met before each federation meeting and decided a 'line' without consulting their local groups. Through this type of organisation they made an explicit attempt to gain control of the city-wide federations. In some areas, they sent 'delegates' to federation meetings from neighbourhoods which didn't have proper groups. At the beginning of the campaign in Avon, for example, there were at least four groups whose contact person didn't live anywhere near the APTU area. In other areas such as Stoke Newington in London, 'Militant' groups were set up in competition with groups which had already been long established. In some cases outsiders were brought in to set up these rival groups:

We set up an Anti-Poll Tax Union on the estate that I lived on. The first meeting was really good. About 40-50 people turned up. But after the fourth meeting, Militant's 'Newport Against The Poll Tax' started organising meetings on the same night as my one. They leafletted the whole estate leaving a blank space around my house.
Mike B, Bettws, South Wales, 3/4/91.

This activity was carried out to ensure that Militant had enough votes in the federation meetings to take control of them and it was not only confined to small areas. Militant set up an alternative federation in London (the London Steering Group of APTUs) in competition with the London Federation of Anti-Poll Tax Unions which had been meeting for some months and already involved most of the established Anti-Poll Tax Unions. This cynical approach created a great deal of resentment and many local group members began to feel that they were being used. As a result, Militant quickly lost the trust of many non-aligned activists who had initially been sympathetic to them because of the work they had done on the ground.

Nevertheless, while keeping this debate well away from the local groups, Militant openly defended their approach on the political circuits:

The truth of the matter is that we all started off in this campaign with an equal opportunity and with the chance to build and argue our arguments and positions in whatever way we chose. Yes, Militant is organised, and of course being organised, being part of a homogeneous political trend, gives you an advantage. You aren't part of a homogeneous organisation or a political trend so that you can become heterogeneous as soon as anyone starts moaning. If you believe in a programme, if you believe in a method... then you have a duty to argue that through to the end and we've done so, we make no apologies for doing that.

Robin Clapp, South West Correspondent, Militant, 24/5/91.

In Avon, the initial response of non-aligned activists was to play them at their own game and make sure that there were enough non-aligned delegates at each meeting to prevent Militant taking control. After about a month, this strategy was abandoned, not because it hadn't worked – it was very effective, but because activists (including myself) felt they were wasting time fighting Militant when they should have been fighting the Poll Tax. We decided that the only way to make the local campaign fully democratic was to make it so big that no political grouping could dominate it. So we went out and spoke to groups of people in every neighbourhood of Avon and created new Anti-Poll Tax Unions. By the end of 1989 there were 50 local Anti-Poll Tax Unions and another 25 affiliated organisations, each entitled to send two delegates. From that point on, the Avon campaign consistently had a majority of non-aligned delegates and, as a result, most of the political groupings began to work well with each other.

A similar response was made in the Birmingham Federation, and with the exception of areas such as Glasgow and Liverpool (where Militant were entrenched), it proved fairly possible to deal with attempts by political parties to take control of the movement (at a regional level) once those activists, who were not politically experienced, had realised what was going on. Even if the federations were difficult to reform because no-one wanted to go to them, all sorts of informal communication networks could be set up. It was more difficult to prevent problems at a national level.

Delegates voting at the second AGM of the Avon Federation of Anti-Poll Tax Unions.

Mark Simmons

In August 1989, a coalition of non-aligned activists, with the support of the London, Norwich and Avon Federations called a meeting for September 3rd to discuss the setting up of a federation for Britain. Invitations were sent out to every known Anti-Poll Tax group. Militant refused to participate in the initiative, and with the support of the Militant-controlled Scottish Federation, called a rival meeting (of twenty regional delegates who they claimed represented the movement) for September 1st. This meeting went ahead and set up a steering committee to organise a national conference for November.

Two days later, 200 people representing around 360 groups met at the Polytechnic of Central London to discuss how to respond. They were furious at Militant's overt attempts to hijack the movement, but felt it was too dangerous to set up an alternative federation and split the movement. They agreed that activists should attend the conference in November and argue an alternative political perspective, but by now most people were fairly cynical because it was obvious that Militant was planning to bus in the whole of its active membership to the conference. Because of this it was decided to set up a group called 3D (which stood for Don't Pay, Don't Collect, Don't Implement) to provide information, technical advice and support for the movement, and to co-ordinate that political activity which the All-Britain Federation would not support. This was not to be an alternative federation, but it did become (along with other groups such as the Trafalgar Square Defendants' Campaign) an alternative centre of national leadership, holding regular activists' workshops and publishing a bi-monthly newsletter.

Over the next months, Militant's 'conference steering group' wrote a draft constitution for the federation and determined who should be allowed to attend the conference. Most non-aligned groups argued that delegation status should be restricted to Anti-Poll Tax Unions because they were the ones fighting the struggle. But Militant selectively chose to allow other groups to be delegates. Labour Party and trade union branches could be delegates, but not SNP, Green Party and SWP branches (all of whom, unlike the Labour Party, had policies supporting non-payment). Their argument was that these groups were 'not part of the labour movement'. As a result, of 1,600 delegates who attended, 546 were from 'other labour movement bodies' – and the vast majority of these were Militant supporters. Even the 'Youth Rights Campaign', a Militant youth organisation was allowed to send delegates. Because of this extraordinarily brazen manipulation, the All-Britain Federation lost what little trust remained of the majority of Anti-Poll Tax activists. Large numbers of non-aligned groups refused to send delegates and, in some regions, virtually all the Anti-Poll Tax groups opted out. In the Eastern Region, for example, none of the major cities, such as Norwich sent delegates from local APTUs.

Despite what had happened, an olive branch was offered to Militant, when 3D included Tommy Sheridan (a charismatic orator who was the Militant chair of the Scottish Federation) on their slate for the three national officers. Militant, once again, declined to support a united front and elected themselves to 13 out of 16 national executive places, including the three national officer positions. Sham Singh, Ian Greaves and I (the three non-aligned executive members) attended national committee meetings – mainly in order to get information out to the rest of the movement, but by then all hope of an effective All-Britain Federation had disappeared. By the time of the second national conference a year later, the number of delegates had dropped from 1,600 to 1,350, while the number of Anti-Poll Tax Unions had trebled. Only 639 APTUs were represented out of a total of well over 1,500 known groups. In the South West Region, of 150 Anti-Poll Tax Unions, only 47 thought it important enough to send even one delegate to the conference, despite the fact that the campaign was at the height of activity.

This lack of respect was strengthened because the All-Britain Federation failed to provide the support the movement needed. Its biggest failure was the lack of information sent out to groups. For example, there was supposed to be a regular newsletter. Ian Greaves (the Yorkshire representative) and I agreed to edit and produce it, but only three were distributed in the first year. We produced another four, but they were either not distributed or not printed by the national officers. They had been 'locked in a room in London' or 'a van had broken down on the motorway'. These problems were bound up with the fact that Militant was a political organisation with a wider political agenda. They didn't produce information from the All-Britain Federation because they wanted the *Militant* newspaper to become the voice of the movement. I was told numerous times by Militant members to stop complaining about the lack of information because if people wanted it they could read *Militant*. This was not an argument which carried much weight with ordinary members of local APTUs waiting for information. These newsletters were the only point of contact most local groups had with the All-Britain Federation , so it is not really surprising that it so quickly became marginal to the movement – most non-Militant groups had no evidence that it existed.

Another example of mismanagement which arose from their determination to work alone was the organisation of the national demonstration on March 31st 1990 (described in detail in the next chapter). Militant executive members estimated that there would only be 20,000 people on the demonstration. The three non-aligned delegates said that it would be more like quarter of a million. This massive mismatch of views can be explained by the difference in group organisation which I described earlier in this section. For, in those areas where the public were meeting regularly together, there had been increasing demands for action for some months. In the Militant controlled groups (where the work was done by the executive), there was not sufficient contact with the public for officers to know what they felt. Given that Militant was basing its assessment solely on its own groups, it is not surprising that it misjudged the mood. The result was that they underestimated the resources which were needed to go into organising the demonstration and failed to collect any money from the 200,000 demonstrators who were there. The future activities of the federation could have been financed for some time to come if only 10p had been collected from each demonstrator. Instead the event made a £12,000 loss and the federation was unable to properly finance *any* future activities. This is a clear illustration of why a diverse (but united) political leadership will always be stronger than a sectarian one.

So, in failing to command the respect of the larger movement, the All-Britain Federation simply became a co-ordination forum for Militant controlled groups. In this respect the Labour Party was right when it sent out its memo to all Labour Party Branches telling that the All-Britain Federation was no more than a Militant Front. What the Labour Party failed to realise was that the All-Britain Federation was virtually irrelevant to the movement.

As a 'federation' it had no direct control over its member groups. It could pass policies and take initiatives, but it was up to the local groups whether they wanted to take part in the them or not. Local groups had the power to do

The power of the movement was in the localities. Stalls like this one in Hackney gave the campaign visibility and provided the public with much needed information.

and say what they wanted and the majority of groups who didn't like the way the All-Britain Federation was organised simply ignored it. Given this, the problems of the All-Britain Federation were never seen as important enough to warrant splitting the movement.

The Anti-Poll Tax campaign was not seriously damaged by political manipulation in the federations because it was a resistance campaign. Unlike protest campaigns which are dependent on media impact and electoral success, this campaign was solely dependent on the actions of *local* people organised into *local* groups. Because there were so many people involved, the political factions simply didn't have the numbers to make a difference at a local level. And because people felt that *they* were in control, they stayed involved. This made the movement strong and highly resistant to political corruption.

4

RIOT AND
REBELLION

Mark Simmons

The Town Hall Demonstrations

The Anti-Poll Tax Unions were built up gradually between early 1989 and February 1990. During this period, most of the movement's public profile was in the neighbourhoods. But, as the date for implementation in England and Wales approached, activity picked up. Demonstrations were called in every region. In early 1990, anger exploded across South-West England. In Plymouth, a demonstration of over 10,000 people was organised by Hilda Biles, a former Tory voter; twelve local women organised a demonstration of 5,000 people in Paignton, Devon; 5,000 demonstrated in Exeter; 1,500 in Bath; 3,000 in Barnstable; 5,000 in Taunton; 1,500 in Stroud; Midsommer Norton and Radstock, with a total population of only 20,000, held a demonstration of 2,000 people. In the months running up

Demonstrators surrounded the Bristol Council House. As they pushed towards the main doors, the police moved in with horses.

Mark Simmons

84

to implementation of the Poll Tax, over 50,000 people from the South-West attended major local demonstrations.

On 6th March 1990, the day the council set the level of the Poll Tax, a demonstration was called in Bristol. 5,000 people gathered on the large green outside the Council House. A rally was in progress when the police decided to move into the back of the crowd, using a snatch squad to arrest one of the demonstrators. The crowd responded in unison:

> The whole crowd turned the other way, and started running towards the police. People grabbed those who had been arrested and pulled them away. The police brought in reinforcements and charged the crowd with horses.
>
> *Danny Burns, extract from diary, 7/3/90.*

This situation was inflamed by police tactics outside the Council House itself:

> The entrance was blocked by four mounted police officers with rows of other officers on foot behind them. The presence of these horses in a crowded area was dangerous and provocative. The officers directed the frightened animals into the crowd, deliberately creating a crush which was aggravated by policemen pushing from the rear.
>
> *Eleanor Porter, letter to the Bristol Evening Post.*

26 people were arrested. Both police and demonstrators were seriously injured. One police officer was kicked unconscious when he tried to make an arrest. Six more were dragged out of their van. PC David Wallis, who had served in Northern Ireland, described the situation as 'worse than Ulster'.

From here, activity spread to the rest of England and Wales. The next day 5,000 protesters massed outside Hackney Town Hall in London. As the police baton-charged the crowd, in an attempt to stop them from entering the council meeting, they were resisted by a hail of bricks, bottles and stones. The demonstration spread up the high street, and a general riot ensued. 50 shop windows were smashed. By the end of the evening, 56 people had been arrested.

Wherever councils met to set the Poll Tax, hundreds of demonstrators were outside. Large demonstrations were held in Newcastle, Lambeth, Southampton, Norwich, Southwark and outside most city Town Halls. Some were peaceful, others were attacked by the police and turned into riots. In many areas demonstrators forced their way into the council chambers and the meetings had to be abandoned.

Kinnock responded as he did in the miners' strike. He said that people didn't deserve to be:

> exploited by Toy Town revolutionaries who pretend that the tax can be stopped and the government toppled simply by non-payment.
>
> *The Guardian, 10/3/90.*

Thatcher and the Tory press blamed the demonstrations on 'rent a mob' extremists but they never revealed where the thousands of demonstrators were rented from.

The Town Hall riots didn't change councils' decisions to implement the tax, but they strengthened the movement by creating an atmosphere of defiance - a spirit of resistance which made its mark in Trafalgar Square less than a month later.

Mark Simmons

86

Riots In Trafalgar Square

We finally arrived in Kennington Park around 11.30. All thoughts of aches and pains went as we saw the people gathering, pensioners, young people, children in push-chairs, several wheelchairs, lots of family groups all in summer clothes enjoying the sun. Some had brought musical instruments and were giving impromptu concerts, the atmosphere was wonderful, no tension, no undercurrents... This was the day the people's voice would be heard.
Mrs. Sylvia Chaffey, St. Annes, Bristol, 31/3/90.

On March 31st 1990, a national demonstration was called by the non-payment campaign. 200,000 people turned up to the march in London and over 50,000 people joined the march in Glasgow. The sun shone for the whole day. The mood of the demonstrators was jubilant. We had been fighting for months on our own, and now everyone was marching together.

People started to gather around mid-day. As ever, they were greeted by the paper-sellers of the revolutionary Left. The park was lined with stalls. Local groups sold pamphlets, stickers and badges. Newsletters describing local campaigns were handed out to the crowd. There were thousands of colourful banners, some intricately woven with images of resistance, others spray-painted with crude slogans: 'Fuck Off Maggie'. Anti-Poll Tax Unions were there from every conceivable locality. Tens of thousands had come from London, thousands more were bused in from all over England and Wales. In Bristol for example some local groups filled over two coaches on their own and in total Bristol sent over 60 coaches. The mixture of people at the demonstration was extraordinary: ex-striking miners; Greater London Pensioners Against The Poll Tax; bedraggled

87

punks mingled amongst the well-dressed middle class. As the park began to fill, the noise level got louder. Musicians were playing Anti-Poll Tax songs. Slogans were being chanted to the rhythmic beat of drums 'Poll Tax, No Way! Don't Collect, Don't Pay!' – 'Break The Law!

Mark Simmons

Not The Poor!', An old man wandered through the crowd holding a home-made placard which read: 'I exist on £47 a week. How can I pay the Poll Tax?'

A campaign bus and a flat bed truck were parked up, one in each field of the park, surrounded by loudspeakers. Speeches were made by activists. Some of the crowd focused intently on what was said, others, disinterested in boring speeches, heckled or wandered to the back of the crowd waiting for the action to start. By 12.30 p.m. there were so many people, it was no longer possible to see the grass. The mood was confident but not aggressive. In each field a vote was taken – a statement of intent that the demonstrators wanted a peaceful march. It

Above:

A massive peaceful

demonstration -

the calm before the storm.

88

looked as if every hand in the park was raised.

The march left the park at around 1.30 p.m. Initially the police took a low profile, but at 3.00 p.m. twenty people staged a peaceful sit down opposite Downing Street. The police carried out two brutal arrests:

> A man in a wheelchair was attacked and arrested by the police, separated from his wheelchair and thrown into a police van. A woman was arrested and, in front of the crowd stripped of her clothes. Both arrests angered and incensed the crowd. It was an obvious police provocation of a peaceful demonstration.
>
> *TSDC, defendants' legal meeting minutes, 27th May.*

300 people sat down, and then the police brought in the horses. Mounted riot police baton-charged the crowd. The crowd, angered by this violent provocation retaliated throwing sticks, banner poles, bottles – anything they could find. Young people, armed only with placards fought hand to hand with police. Some demonstrators were batoned down with truncheons, others had riot shields thrust into their faces. As the missiles began to rain down the police retreated:

> The violence seemed to be following us around. Pedestrian isles were being torn up and real serious lumps of concrete being thrown at the romper-suited police. I found myself with rock in hand. The first I threw was aimed at a group of police. I watched it bounce off a shield. My second rock was more specifically aimed at their front line. Again, it was well-deflected. I saw a rock strike a policeman's visor and he didn't even blink. The police were shielding themselves from the missiles raining down, but they were vulnerable to rocks aimed at their legs and midriffs. The police were taking a battering. Every now and then a policeman would crumple to his knees and the crowd would roar.
>
> *Rioter, New Statesman, 6/4/90.*

Some cops kept their wits about them and
tried to slow the retreat but most just put
their heads down and ran into kicks and
punches. Those that fell were dragged
away along the ground by their colleagues.
Poll Tax Riot pamphlet, 1990.

From 4.00 p.m. for over an hour, the police
tried to force people out of Whitehall into Trafalgar Square with violent baton charges. At
5.00 p.m. the sky turned from blue to grey.
Flames started to pour out of the Higgs and Hill
Building on Trafalgar Square. Someone had
climbed into the portakabins on the front of the
building and set them alight. For a while, the
whole sky seemed to be on fire. The crowd
watched, mesmerised:

Flames from the burning portakabins leapt
into the sky and smoke billowed towards
Nelson's Column. Flames were also seen
coming from the ground floor of South
Africa House... firemen using jets and two
turn-table ladders fought the blaze for three
hours.
The Observer, 1/4/90.

The heat began to rise again when the police
started to drive vans into the crowd:

We saw a white police van, which seemed
to come from nowhere, drive down the
road so fast we only had time to turn our
eyes... to see it hit several people... I
screamed and we ran behind the barriers as
another van careered down the road,
hitting a man down before our very eyes. I
was absolutely shocked. I am normally a
quiet person but this incensed me. I began
shouting at them. Angeline had to hold my
T-shirt pulling me back.
Bristol woman, letter to Dawn Primarolo MP, April 1990.

At the time I was standing on a black lion at the
foot of Nelson's column. I surveyed the whole
scene. Three to four police vehicles emerged
from the Strand, travelling at speed – about 30-

40 miles an hour. They literally cut through the crowd and there was nowhere for those in the way to go :

> As I looked up the length of the road, I saw a police van speeding towards us. I got out of the road and watched in horror as it sped in towards the crowd and screeched to a halt... a body flew through the air and landed in a heap on the side of the road. This was too much, my anger exploded and I ran towards the van screaming and shouting and pulled open the door on the driver's side, screaming blue murder as the terrified officer inside wrenched the door closed. I spat, I banged on the windows... looking for something to throw, something to hit with. Everything was happening at once, the man in the road with people bending over him, people crying, me shouting... a woman gently rocked her baby, rhythmically, protectively, as she made her way across the road away from the violence.
> *Poll Tax Riot pamphlet, April 1990.*

Some demonstrators bravely ran up to the vans and covered the windscreens with their hands in an attempt to stop them. One was mown down and dragged along the ground by the police riot van. Another van reversed without warning into the densely-packed crowd. Missiles were thrown at them and about 70 people, enraged by these attacks, surrounded one of the vans and attempted to wedge barriers underneath it to prevent more people from being injured. They failed, and the police attack continued. A demonstrator picked up a metal scaffolding pole and hurled it through the window. It glanced the head of the driver and went out through the other side.

As the violent confrontations spread across Trafalgar Square, wave upon wave of mounted police charged the crowd:

> I saw horses charge up the steps of St. Martin-in-the-Fields, where young children

had been taken, supposedly out of harm's way. They made no attempt to disperse the crowd peacefully. They just came charging in.

Eleanor Mills, The Independent, 2/4/90.

The police were out of control, some thriving on the tension, others terrified:

It got worse, and I was frightened. The adrenalin took over. I tried to hurt them, to stop them hurting me. I felt like crying, but couldn't. I wanted to go home to leave them to it, but I couldn't.

Paddy Collins, Police Tactical Support Group, Metline – magazine of the Metropolitan Police Federation, September 1990.

As the evening wore on, the crowds were separated, and moved in smaller groups throughout the West End. Cars were over-turned and shop windows smashed. Discriminating attacks were made on BMWs and Volvos, rich fur shops and jewellers. Other places were damaged too but, as I walked up Regent Street that evening, it was clear that most of the damage was against symbols of wealth.

Hundreds of people ran down the middle of roads, diving between the static cars. The task for the police got harder as it began to get dark. It was almost impossible to tell the tourists from the demonstrators. The police didn't take much care to distinguish. A woman sat on the curb with blood streaming from her head. She had been truncheoned down by the police because she had tried to pass through their lines to get out of the area. She had only come to the West End to do some shopping. Tourists wandered around bewildered. A Japanese man emerged from the Underground station at Piccadilly Circus and asked me, 'Does this happen often?'

Opposite:

A badly injured

demonstrator is led away

by a concerned friend.

By the end of the day, 341 people had been arrested and thousands were injured. According to the police debriefing (March 1991) 542 police officers were wounded:

Mark Simmons

Mark Simmons

Mark Simmons

More than 100 police officers were treated in mobile hospital wagons behind Whitehall at the height of the riot.
The Observer, 1/4/90.

The number of civilian injuries was never recorded. The arrests didn't stop on March 31st. Over the following days, the police, under the control of Commander Roy Ramm set up Operation Carnaby. Its aim was to track down everyone who had 'committed offences' who were not arrested on the day. The police had 90 hours of video footage and 30,000 still photos. They drafted in 137 detectives and 12 solicitors to work on them full-time with a brief to investigate 18,307 offences.

Operation Carnaby used the gutter press to do its work. Papers paraded 'mugshots' of demonstrators, with headlines such as 'Hunt the Rioters', 'If You Know 'em, SHOP 'EM'. *The People* newspaper of May 13th displayed the faces of eight men 'on the most wanted list of police':

Man 1: Wearing T-shirt inscribed 'Freedom, Justice, Peace.' Pictured in St. Martin's Lane demonstrating his love for peace by smashing cars with an iron bar and hurling bricks at the police.

Man 2: Dark brown hair and moustache. Wanted for serious assaults on police.

Man 8: Swarthy Latin or Mediterranean type with high forehead, unkempt brown hair. He is wanted in connection with the attempted murder of a policeman when a 20lb scaffold pole was hurled through the front window of a police car like a spear.

Do you know any of these rioters? If so, give us a call now...

The pictures of all those described were spread across the front cover and inside front pages. This was 'trial by media' presenting a

Opposite

Above: The use of riot

horses is supposed to be a

last resort tactic, but on

March 31st they led the

assault.

Below: Theatre-land

hoardings provide appro-

priate comment on the

day's events. 'Fast, furious

and very very funny;

British farce at its best;

Superbly demented; A

night to remember.'

completely biased and distorted image of what happened. The example of 'Man 8' is a case in point. As I have described earlier, he was trying to stop a police van which was travelling at over 30 miles an hour through a densely-packed crowd which had nowhere to move to. Scores of innocent by-standers had been seriously injured, some lying on the ground bleeding. In attempting to stop the van before it killed someone, this man was committing an act of great courage, yet he was accused by the press of attempted murder before he had even come to trial. Three of these men were later found not guilty by the courts.

17 photographs were published which led to 13 arrests. Detective Chief Superintendent Roy Ramm said that 'we have so far identified close to 300 people caught on film clearly committing serious offences. We intend to carry on until we have traced all of them'.

Operation Carnaby didn't intend to 'trace' them all however, they only needed to find people who roughly fitted the bill. This is demonstrated by the way the police carried out their 'dawn raids'.

On Thursday 21st June at 6.00 a.m. they violently broke into six flats in Stoke Newington, London. All the occupants were members of the Homleigh Road Estate Anti-Poll Tax Union. Eleven were arrested. That day the local group put out a statement of what had happened:

> In one flat, Anne Marie who's just come out of hospital with her ten day old baby was awoken as her door was sledge-hammered in... eight cops rushed down the hall, assaulted her and pushed her into the bedroom still undressed, as they attacked and arrested her partner, Sam. He was taken away with his head bleeding. No cautioning, no warrants, no warning. The phone was kicked to 'stop you ringing for support'. The cops ripped out pages of her address book, took away her photos and said, in explanation, 'Poll Tax Riot'.
>
> Alan, another local activist, lives on his

own. Cops broke down his door, hand-cuffed him, smashed up his flat, floor, carpet, heating ducts, phone, kitchen-ware and stereo. He was arrested. The local police attempted to justify the raid saying that 'the whole area is an anarchist hot-bed'.

Operation Carnaby provided an excuse for the police to intimidate known local activists.

This aggressive response was also reflected in the police media campaign. The police officer responsible for the march, Deputy Assistant Commissioner David Meynell said:

The tabloids were eager to

do the government's dirty

work. Similar spreads were

displayed in most of the

popular newspapers

I have never seen such sustained and savage violence used directly against the police. There was no pretence, it was a simple and brutal assault upon my officers.
The Guardian, 2/4/90.

The police declared that there were only 40,000 demonstrators on the march. Yet Trafalgar Square, which has a capacity of 60,000, was full to overflowing before the end of the march had left Kennington Park. It was in their interest to underestimate the size of the march. If it seemed smaller, then it could be written off as a demonstration of political activists, not part of a mass movement, and the aggressive tactics of the police would appear more legitimate.

In addition to Operation Carnaby, an internal riot debriefing team was set up by Deputy Commissioner John Metcalfe. It:

consisted of 13 full-time officers. They interviewed 1,445 people over a period of several months, analysing information

Alan's flat, after the police had finished with it. Six months later his charges were dropped because even after turning his flat upside down, they had no evidence.

obtained on the Home Office Large Major
Enquiry System to determine the sequence
of events and catalogue suggestions made.
Questions were asked about planning,
briefing and initial deployment, incidents
and police operations before, during and
after disorder broke out, injuries, equipment, communications, transport welfare
and support.
Metropolitan Police debriefing, March 1991.

A year later they produced a twenty page report. But despite all the time and resources
available to the debriefing team, it didn't contain a single mention of casualties sustained by
the public (three pages were devoted to police
casualties). Yet, in Bristol, one demonstrator
was in hospital for six months after the riot and
is expected to be paralysed for life. Many suffered serious head wounds (some who I know
personally). Television footage showed demonstrators mown down by police vans and
trampled by police horses and overall, there
was a higher number of casualties sustained by
the demonstrators than the police. In the introduction to his report, John Metcalfe states:

There are few places in the world where
rioting on this scale would have been
brought under control without loss of life or
the use of draconian measures by the
police.

The fact that no-one lost their life was a miracle.
It was not a result of sensitive policing. It was a
testament to the responsibility of the crowd,
who shepherded older people and children out
of harm's way, and who actively defended
themselves against police brutality. If the demonstrators hadn't fought back in such a determined way, there is little doubt that someone
would have been killed. If driving riot vans
through thick crowds at 30-miles an hour is not
draconian then what is? The police acknowl-
edged in their report that these police vehicles:

raised the temperature of the crowd and

> coincided with an increase in the level of violence directed towards the police... Police vehicles should avoid travelling through large crowds in congested areas to reduce the possibility of escalating violence.

but they refused to take any responsibility for the events which took place. Despite the numbers of injuries to demonstrators and the police atrocities captured on film, not a single police officer was prosecuted for their role on that day. Furthermore, senior officers took no responsibility for their failure to take action before the march.

When it became obvious that the demonstration was going to be much larger than the All-Britain Federation had anticipated, they requested that the destination of the march be changed to Hyde Park. This was declined by the Department of the Environment and the police, on the technical grounds that they had received less than a weeks notice. The fact that they knew they were sending 200,000 people into a space which had a capacity of only 60,000 suggests that the police attack was premeditated. If they hadn't wanted a riot they would have diverted the march to Hyde Park. This is another reason why it was in their interest to suggest that there were only 40,000 people on the march. This strategy didn't even satisfy the police who were at the front line:

> I'll tell you what really got up my nose – the senior officers who let us take the 'treatment', and then publicly praised our restraint and fortitude in the face of abuse and violence, and then quoted the numbers of injured officers as a measure of their courage.
>
> Paddy Collins, Metline – *magazine of the Metropolitan Police Federation, September 1990.*

The government tried to establish that the violence was pre-planned by extremists. Copies of the anarchist paper *Class War* were displayed to prove that there were elements in the crowd who were out to incite violence. They didn't mention that Class War and other groups have produced similar literature at every demonstration for the last ten years.

The Tower Hamlets Arts Project produced some interesting evidence to the contrary. They showed that it was ordinary people who were involved, and almost all had been provoked. Instead of focusing their cameras on 'the action' as the media did, they focused on sections of the crowd. They captured ordinary people listening to the rally in Trafalgar Square unaware that anything was going on in Whitehall. They recorded a change of atmosphere as the noise of the riot filtered through to the Square. At this point people turned their attention away from the rally and watched the riot. When the riot got closer and they could see the police atrocities, they started to shout and, as the police advanced and threatened them personally, they began to pick up sticks and bottles and throw them. This was not premeditated violence, it was a progressive response to the actions of the police.

But it was necessary for the government to make out that the riot was caused by extremists. Their political strategy was similar to that which they employed during the miners strike. The miners too, were forced to respond to violence with violence and were then labelled as extremists. The government aided by Kinnock used this to drive a wedge down the middle of the labour movement which diminished support from other national unions, and gradually broke the miners' unity. Thatcher hoped to do the same with the Anti-Poll Tax campaign. By getting the Labour Party to denounce the violence, she hoped to split the Anti-Poll Tax movement down the middle. There was a clear attempt to link the violence with non-payment:

> If you tell people to break the law by not paying the tax, you're not far off telling them to break other laws as well.
> Norman Tebbit, Conservative Party Chair, 2/6/90.

The Tories tried to give the impression that

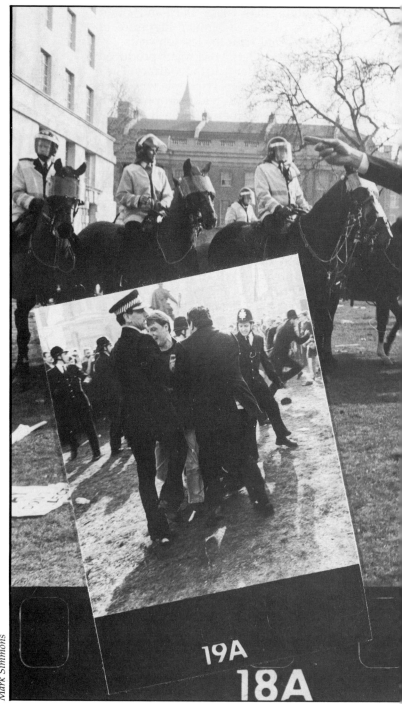

Mark Simmons

ordinary people on the demonstration had been manipulated by non-payers. They declared that the non-payers had now been exposed for what they were, and called on those who rejected violence to reject non-payment. Kinnock quickly fell into line, saying that those responsible for violence should be treated as criminals:

> I regard them and treat them as enemies of freedom.
> The Guardian, 2/4/90.

But the Tories didn't realise how big the Anti-Poll Tax movement was. They assumed that its base was in the labour movement and they were wrong. As a result Kinnock's words didn't make any difference. Nor did the defensive statements made by Tommy Sheridan, the Chair of the All-Britain Federation, who said in a hastily called press conference, immediately after the march:

> The majority of those who became embroiled in the running battles had nothing to do with our protest.

Sheridan feared the response of the public. Yet the first opinion poll to be carried out after the riot, showed that well over a third of people openly condoned the demonstrators fight-back against the police. The riot exposed the role of the police and was hailed by the foreign press as the end of Thatcherism. It clearly indicated how strongly people felt about the tax, and in its wake the Labour Party (ironically) gained its strongest lead in the opinion polls. Perhaps more important than all of this, the number of Anti-Poll Tax Unions trebled within weeks of March 31st.

Overleaf:

Police spokesmen blamed

hot headed frontline officers

for 'isolated incidents' of

gratuitous violence, but the

photographic evidence

shows that this was orches-

trated by senior officers.

The Defendants And
The Trials

The atmosphere was electric and extremely
sober at the first meeting. People realised
that this was an immense task which was
going to be taken on.

You gain respect if you concentrate on your
basic activity and do it effectively. We
concentrated on our basic work and won
the whole of the Anti-Poll Tax movement
over to the TSDC. We allied ourselves with
the movement, rather than any tendency
within it.

Dave Morris, Trafalgar Square Defendants' Campaign,
25/4/91.

Building A Defendants' Campaign

341 people were arrested on March 31st. Another 150 were arrested as a result of Operation
Carnaby. Most were charged under the Public
Order Act. No legal preparation had been carried out by the All-Britain Federation. As a
result, people who had never been arrested
before, some facing charges of Riot (Section 1)
or Violent Disorder (Section 2) with possible
prison sentences of up to ten years, had to face
the police with no idea of their rights.

When Steve Nally and Tommy Sheridan
denounced those involved in the riot and
threatened to hold an internal enquiry and
expel from the movement any person or organisation which was responsible, many in the
movement felt betrayed:

We are going to hold our own internal
inquiry which will go public and if necessary name names.

Steve Nally, ITN, April 1st.

Our federation is going to be conducting

an internal inquiry to try and root out the
trouble-makers.
Tommy Sheridan, LWT news, April 1st.

Groups and federations from across Britain
condemned the statements. Even the Lothian
Federation, which had often supported the
leadership of the All-Britain Federation,
passed a motion of censure against them. After
the statements of Steve Nally and Tommy
Sheridan, the All-Britain Federation was not in
a position to mount a defence campaign which
could gain the confidence of the movement (let
alone the defendants). This was a serious situation, because if people didn't feel they would
be properly defended, they would be reluctant
to come on future demonstrations, and those
who had been arrested needed immediate
practical support. An organisation needed to
be formed to do the job that the All-Britain
Federation was unwilling to do.

The initiative to form an independent defendants' campaign developed out of informal
discussions between people involved in the 3D
communications network, such as Terri
Conway (Islington APTU) and Dave Morris
(Tottenham APTU) – and two others: Sean
Waterman, who had been involved in the
Broadwater Farm Defence Campaign, and
Alistair Mitchell, who was a defendant. They
decided to call a meeting at the Conway Hall in
London. The meeting was well-attended by
defendants and it quickly became clear that a
serious systematic campaign was needed to get
good legal advice to defendants, monitor all the
court cases and fight the image of the demonstration which had been put about, by exposing
the police attack. The meeting drew up a nine-
point programme for action:

The campaign will:

1 Unconditionally defend of all those
   arrested on March 31st.
2 Be controlled by and be accountable
   to the defendants.
3 Be totally independent of any other

organisation.

4 Seek support from the whole Anti-Poll Tax movement and all other sympathetic organisations.

5 Seek to co-ordinate the legal defence of all those arrested.

6 Seek to build a coherent picture of events of 31/3/90 from the point of view of those arrested.

7 Publicise the points of view of defendants.

8 Raise money for a bust fund, controlled by the defendants to cover their legal and welfare costs.

9 Ensure that at all future Anti-Poll Tax events there will be proper legal cover and support for anyone arrested. This will include an office and workers to visit places of detention and look after prisoners' welfare.

TSDC newsletter, May 1990.

The leadership of the All-Britain Federation was not happy that an initiative had been taken outside of their control and immediately issued a statement to the Anti-Poll Tax movement calling for donations to a defence fund and campaign:

They thought that if they could raise the money then they could call the tune. But it was a destructive move because there was already a defence campaign which had been set up under the control of defendants. Apart from the fact that the All-Britain Federation had no experience of defence campaigns and their lack of enthusiasm, they were also the same people who had condemned the demonstrators for fighting back against the police and causing trouble. It's quite obvious that a large section of the defendants wouldn't have any confidence in something which was run by those people.

Dave Morris, 25/4/91.

But by the time the All-Britain Federation

called its first meeting on May 12th, the Trafalgar Square Defendants' Campaign had issued it's first newsletter, had held regular meetings of 20-30 defendants and had monitored the courts for three weeks. Only two new defendants turned up to the Federation defendants' meeting and, by the end of it, the All- Britain Federation was forced to support the Trafalgar Square Defendants' Campaign.

This was a significant achievement because they disagreed in principle with two of the TSDC's fundamental aims. They didn't like the idea of a campaign which was accountable to the defendants – because they wouldn't be able to control it, and they didn't like the idea of unconditional support for all defendants.

Mark Simmons

The TSDC argued that unconditional support for all defendants was the only basis on
which a unified campaign could be built:

You can't say, we support these people and
not those people, or we support these
people a bit and those people a lot. The
consequences of this would have been
disastrous. The most important aspect of a
defendants' campaign is not setting one
group off against another. You can't create
an organisation, a struggle, a campaign
without a strong feeling of solidarity, unity
and mutual respect... You can't say the
ones who were 'innocent', i.e. framed, are
more important than the ones who were
'guilty' but were actually defending themselves, and that they are both more important than those who hate the police anyway because of their experience.
Dave Morris, 25/4/91.

The TSDC believed that it was not their job
to make judgments about who was politically
correct. Everyone had different views and per-
spectives and should have equal access to the
decision-making process, to funding where it
was available and to legal support. The views
of each defendant were respected:

If some people hate the police that much
that they want to have a go at them at
every opportunity, that's not because
they're born that way, or they're sent from
Mars, it's because the police have created
that feeling in the population by the way
they have acted.
Dave Morris, 25/4/91.

The first task for the TSDC was to track
down all the defendants. In the beginning they
only had hearsay and newspaper evidence to
go on. *The Sunday Mirror* published a list of all
those who were arrested – obviously provided
by the police. This was useful as a checklist, but
it was extremely difficult to make contact with
all the defendants:

Opposite:

Riot police in disarray as

buildings start to burn.

109

Initially ten people were heard on one day. If proper legal backup had been done on the demonstration we could have reached every defendant in the first week. But by about the second month when we really got going, people were appearing in twos and threes, it was a race against time because people were getting spread out.
Dave Morris, 25/4/91.

About a dozen people volunteered to carry out the court monitoring process. They attended every hearing, systematically took notes of everything that was said, recorded the numbers of police officers and approached the defendants asking them to attend the now weekly TSDC meetings. These meetings were attended by both supporters and defendants but if controversial issues were discussed the defendants had a veto in the meeting. A series of national defendants' meetings were called which were attended by about 50 defendants. By the summer, over 250 of the defendants had been contacted.

The TSDC ran advice sessions on prison, produced legal briefing notes and mailed out the minutes of the weekly meetings to every defendant every week. A solicitors' group was established with a core of three, but at the peak of early activity they managed to get over fifteen solicitors involved. This proved important because the solicitors' group managed to get hold of over 50 hours of police videos and handed them over to the campaign. The police videos were crucial in getting a lot of people off, and a number of people in the campaign worked extremely hard editing videos and re-jigging them for particular trials. The solicitors' group also got the Crown Prosecution Service to hand over a full list of all of the defendants and the names and addresses of their lawyers. The lawyers were all contacted and, although many were initially reluctant to co-operate with the campaign, they soon realised that TSDC had a lot of information which their clients needed.

In July 1990, the Haldane Society of Socialist Lawyers offered their Central London Office to the campaign. Appeals for money were made across the movement but, although most groups or their federations affiliated, they didn't supply the steady stream of money which was needed. Nevertheless, 25-30 benefit gigs were held within the first couple of months and, by August, the campaign was organised and ready to deal with the more serious crown court cases.

Most of the charges which people faced were under section one, two or three of the Public Order Act (Riot, Violent Disorder and Affray). The more serious charges were subject to a jury trial. The authorities who were nervous about subjecting the demonstration to scrutiny by juries attempted to get defendants to 'plea bargain', offering to drop section two charges if defendants' pleaded guilty to a section three charge. Dropping the charges down meant that people could only be heard in a magistrates' court. In the event, a much higher percentage of the serious charges heard by juries were won by the defendant than those held in the magistrates' courts.

It was clear from the start that the police had fabricated much of their evidence. In one case, in November 1990, a jury used a rare legal power to stop the trial of a man accused of beating up a policeman. A witness, who had been taken away in the same van as Mr. Hanney (the defendant) corroborated his testimony, saying that, in fact, it was he who had been beaten up – by the police!:

[PC Egan] hit him repeatedly. At some stages he changed to punching him with his right hand because the man was trying to cover his head. It went on for at least three minutes.

A medical report confirmed that he had bruising to his forehead, eyebrows and back, and a loss of sensation in his arm.

The statements which the police produced in court were supposed to be independent accounts of what happened. PC Egan theoreti-

Mark Simmons

Mark Simmons

cally wrote his statement at Rochester Row, at 6.45 p.m., while PC Ramsay made his at City Road more than three hours later:

PC EGAN: We were deployed on a short shield cordon attempting to push a violent crowd of 500 plus north in Charing Cross Rd., WC1. All the time we were under prolonged attack of missiles consisting of bricks, bottles, pieces of concrete and coins. The order was given to charge into the extremely violent crowd. As we moved forward I saw a man whom I now know to be Roy Hanney. He was wearing an army-type jacket which was zipped up, and he had closely shaven fair hair. As he came to the front of the crowd, I saw him shouting at us which I couldn't hear due to the noise of the crowd. I then saw Hanney pull his right arm back and throw what appeared to be a lump of concrete into the police cordon

PC RAMSAY: We were deployed as a short shield unit forming a cordon attempting to push violent crowd of about 500 plus north in Charing Cross Road. We were under constant fire from numerous missiles including brick, bottles, sticks and metal bars. The order was given to charge into a violent crowd. As we moved forward, I noticed a man I now know to be Roy Hanney. He had a close cropped head and an army combat jacket on. He came to the forefront of the crowd shouting and swearing at us. I couldn't make out what he was saying but he shouted in an aggressive manner. I then noticed him draw back his right arm and throw what appeared to be a brick into the police cordon. Myself and PC Egan ran forward with other officers towards Hanney.
The Observer, 11/11/90.

The police tried to suggest that any similarities were coincidental but, when the defence asked to see PC Ramsay's handwritten original it showed that 'shaven' had been crossed out and substituted with 'close cropped'. Most of the

Opposite

Above: Confusion at the

heart of the riot.

Below: A worried police

officer looks out of the

smashed window of her riot

van.

jurors responded with open laughter and in the middle of the trial they sent a note to the judge which said they had discussed the case briefly in the courtroom lift and were '...unanimously convinced of the defendant's innocence.' (*The Observer*, 11/11/90). The judge stopped the trial.

In another case, a police officer claimed to have seen a protester throw a brick through the window of South African Airways. Under interrogation he admitted he was 80 yards away in near darkness and he had identified the wrong building. This case was also thrown out of court (*Stand Firm*, January 1991). In a case which was heard in July 1991 a student, Neil Fernandez, was charged with arson attacks on a Porsche 944 and a Jaguar XJ6. *The Guardian* reported:

> The police officer's account of the timing of the three incidents was inaccurate. For the PC to have seen his client near the Porsche in St. Martins Lane, he would have had to have been able to see around a street corner, through railings and over a clump of trees.
> The Guardian, 17/7/91.

The judge said that he would be referring evidence to the Director of Public Prosecutions saying 'There is a police officer in my mind who has committed perjury.' He too dismissed the case.

While it was clear that many defendants had been framed, others who *had* fought back against the police bravely stood up for what they had done. Tim Donaghy, who was charged with Violent Disorder, said at the end of his trial:

> The prosecuting barrister tried to convince the jury that this is just another criminal proceeding. Hell, no! The question that must be asked is 'Who broke which law and for what reason?' If I stand charged with riot and violent disorder, surely the frenzied baton wielding riot cops should stand alongside me? But no! The law

protects a maniac who attacks the innocent indiscriminately with a horse or a van or a baton as long as he wears a blue uniform.

I will neither condone nor feel remorse for what happened. The only possible course of action for us on that demonstration was to do as we did. What does upset me is that the last strands of democracy in this country are rotting. What hope is there for any of us if there is no way to peacefully oppose government policy?

Tim was sent to prison for three years but another case (which was heard in July 1991), went very differently. Michael Conway, a student and ex-miner, was cleared of Violent Disorder after claiming that he had acted in self-defence in order to protect the crowd from police baton charges. He admitted in open court that he had thrown missiles at the police and was shown on video doing so:

Mr. Conway admitted throwing four or five rocks. He said of one incident 'I didn't think this any different to self defence. The whole point is the police caused this.' He admitted digging up part of the road to get more ammunition to throw, but said, 'I didn't walk away because I took a decision to defend the people behind me.'
The Guardian, 18/7/91.

Not only did the jury openly back his stand, but the judge also seemed to be sympathetic. In his summing up statement he said:

Is he the sort of man who would make a decision as to what he was going to do, or is he the sort of man who could have acted impulsively in self defence bearing in mind the need to save himself from further attack and to save others?
The Guardian, 18/7/91.

This judgement came just a month after 39 miners were given £500,000 compensation for assault following the riot at Orgreave in 1985;

the investigation into the West Midlands Serious Crimes Squad; police compensation for violent attacks at the 'Battle of the Beanfield' – Stonehenge; the release of the Birmingham Six and the Guildford Four; and serious doubts about the Broadwater Farm murder conviction. It supported growing historical evidence of police corruption. It was now common knowledge that the police made up evidence in order to secure convictions, and that they were prepared to attack demonstrators in protection of the State.

The lessons of the these struggles are clear. If unarmed demonstrators are provoked and attacked by the police with batons, riot shields, horses or vans driving through crowds, they have the right to fight back. If, in some cases, this means digging up the road and throwing concrete blocks, then so be it. Often attack is the only effective form of defence and, as a movement, we should not be ashamed or defensive about these actions, we should be proud of those who did fight back.

The People's March Against The Poll Tax

After the events in Trafalgar Square, many activists pressed the All-Britain Federation to organise a follow up demonstration in Central London to reassert the right to demonstrate. Their response was inadequate. Five months later they called a 'People's March Against The Poll Tax'. The idea was modelled on the Jarrow Hunger March of the 1930s and more recently the 'People's March for Jobs'. People were to march in three legs from Glasgow, Liverpool and South Wales to London. It was suggested that they would symbolise the struggle against the Poll Tax. But, instead of a mass march involving the whole movement (which we had envisaged), it was to be restricted to 25 people from each starting point. Each marcher was to

116

be kitted out with over £200 worth of track suit, shoes and underwear. This meant raising vast sums of money in advance, organising accommodation and transport for the marchers and calling demonstrations to send them off – a huge work-load to place on a movement which was having to gear up to the court cases which were beginning.

Of the 75 marchers who finally took to the road, over 70 were supporters of the Militant Tendency. The march went ahead on Sunday September 9th. The marchers stopped off at towns and cities along the way and spoke at meetings which were arranged for their arrival. Jeannette McGuin who was one of only three non-Militant marchers on the Glasgow to London leg, left the march disillusioned, returning home after only three and a half weeks. She was

Above:

If only the march had been

as good as the banner.

117

consistently excluded from the decision-making and from speaking on the tour, and was disappointed that most of the people who the march talked to were already supporters of Militant (interview, 9/5/91). She was also surprised that so few of those on the march came from Scotland, even though it was supposed to symbolise a Scottish rebellion. In the end, the Welsh leg of the march became the South-West leg, because the Welsh Federation was inundated with court support work and was forced to pull out. Bristol was asked to send off the march and organise a demonstration at less than two weeks' notice and, as a result this leg was even more shambolic than the Glasgow leg.

The People's March was a purely symbolic action. Such actions can only work if they get a lot of publicity and with the exception of a piece in *The Independent* magazine, this one didn't. The All-Britain Federation claimed that there was a news black-out, yet news items related to the court cases were printed and broadcast every day. The heart of the problem was that the march didn't enthuse people because the participants were a hand-picked club of 75 people. Ordinary people couldn't engage with it, because they had no role and consequently the press didn't pick up on it as an important event. The Anti-Poll Tax movement was successful precisely because it rejected this elitist form of organisation

Brixton, October 20th 1990

While the shortcomings of the march could be accommodated, a bigger problem was that it was seen by Militant as an alternative to a major London demonstration. The Trafalgar Square Defendants' Campaign, The South-West Anti-Poll Tax Federation, and many other groups and federations argued that we had to be seen to be back on the streets and that, if nothing else, the arrival of the People's March in London could be used as a focus for a national demonstration. They also argued that the defendants needed a much higher profile. This argument was rejected by the All-Britain Federation, whose only concession was that if London wanted to organise a demonstration they would not object. After a great deal of heated argument London agreed to organise a rally in Brockwell Park, Brixton for October 20th. But they were not interested in giving a high profile to the defendants. The route they chose didn't go past any of the courts; the publicity didn't mention the defendants or raise the issue of the right to demonstrate. This meant that something else had to be organised.

The Trafalgar Square Defendants' Campaign called for three events. Firstly on October 19th, the day before the Brixton demonstration,

they called for an international day of action. Pickets were held in 15 countries. French demonstrators occupied the British Consulate; an Anti-Poll Tax demonstration was held in Switzerland during a visit of Margaret Thatcher; Dutch activists called a week of action against the Poll Tax which included benefit gigs, film shows and a demonstration outside the offices of British Airways. Pickets were called in Austria, Melbourne, Oslo and the USA.

Above: Polish activists demonstrate outside the British embassy on the international day of action.

119

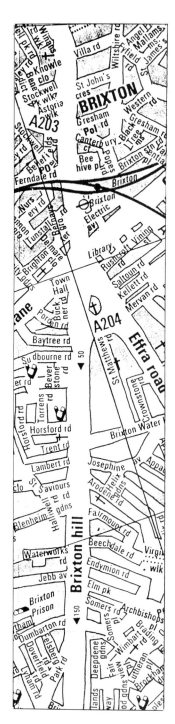

On the day of the demonstration the Trafalgar Square Defendants' Campaign called for a morning picket of Horseferry Rd. magistrates' court which would march to the Brockwell Park rally and then march on to Brixton for a picket outside the jail, where most of the Poll Tax prisoners were being held. The morning event was successful. Over 1,500 people turned up, demonstrated and marched peaceably to the Park – the largest court picket since the second world war. The rally itself attracted 25,000 people (which considering it hadn't been backed by the National Federation was remarkable) and at 3.45 p.m., 3,500 demonstrators set out on the march to Brixton Prison.

As soon as the demonstration left the park the atmosphere changed. The police had earmarked the people participating in the prison picket as the trouble-makers. Whereas they had lightly policed the rest of the day, the march to Brixton was saturated with police officers – 3,000 of them (almost more police than demonstrators). To put this in context: on March 31st when 200,000 people took to the streets, there were only 2,000 police.

The route was lined by three layers of police on either side. The songs of the demonstrators were optimistic and upbeat, but there was a strong air of anticipation. There were rumours flying around that the police wanted a rematch for March 31st. The police officer responsible for overseeing the march (Deputy Assistant Commissioner Metcalfe) had told the march organisers the night before the demonstration that he too had heard 'rumblings' to this effect.

As early as 4.10 p.m. one of the legal liaison volunteers heard PC MS112 shouting (so that the demonstrators could hear): 'I'd like to start kicking some people's heads in now.' Not only were the demonstrators hemmed in, but the march stewards were prevented from crossing police lines. This made communication extremely difficult, especially as the van with the demonstration PA and megaphones hadn't been allowed by the police to join the march. As the march reached the prison it was still in good spirits, the chants were about the Poll Tax and

not the police. The march stopped on the opposite side of the road to the prison and gradually
the police built up the numbers of their cordons
on each side of the picket. Police Support Units
(riot formations) were also deployed in an open
show of strength. At 4.40, for no apparent reason the police officers cordoned off Elm Park,
splitting a number of demonstrators away
from the main march. This was carried out just
twenty minutes after the head of the march
reached the prison, a clear indication that the
police had decided to disperse the picket despite the fact that there was no public order
problem. Two minutes later, the police attacked the crowd:

> The PSUs deployed in front of the church-
> yard push forward into the crowd, attack-
> ing demonstrators with violent and indis-
> criminate use of baton. There is much
> shouting and confusion, and a total of four
> cans are thrown at the surging police. After
> 20-30 seconds, the police resume their
> positions in front of the churchyard and the
> crowd becomes calm again.
>
> *Preliminary report on the policing of the Anti-Poll Tax*
> *Demonstration of October 20th, Trafalgar Square Defendants'*
> *Campaign.*

Given the police provocation, and the fact that
the only provocative action from any of the
demonstrators had been to throw a couple of
empty cans, this was a remarkably restrained
response from the crowd – particularly as
many had first-hand experience of the police
brutality in Trafalgar Square.

At 4.46, the police cleared the forecourt of
the George V pub not allowing people to finish
their drinks. The police were then seen to pick
up the glasses and smash them on the floor.
One was overheard saying 'This is it!' At about
the same time I was passing through a line of
police and heard a similar statement:

> Just wait until it gets dark, then the real fun
> will start.

By 4.50, the police in Endymion Rd. had been seen putting on their riot gear. At 4.55, a police officer was heard to say 'Clear area – shield officers will be deployed'. A group of TSDC stewards intervened in an attempt to block any attack, but a few minutes later 50 police officers charged into the crowd.

Dave Morris one of the main organisers of the demonstration was truncheoned over the head from behind, despite wearing a highly visible fluorescent pink steward's vest. By now the police were out of control:

16.58. Demonstrator lying on road with split head arrested (WL). Two demonstrators carrying Woman M with head wound toward ambulance in the clear lane of Brixton Hill. Police prevent woman M from entering ambulance. Man objects and is arrested.

17.05. Riot police in cordon across Brixton Hill North of Endymion Road shout 'We're on' (RM) and charge (LW). In this charge, young male arrested and handed to officers by the side. PC took him to van and was heard to say 'I don't know what I'm arresting him for.' Senior officer replied 'Arrest him for assault on a PC' The two officers were TW5 and YF143.

TSDC report on the October 20th demonstration.

[letters in brackets are initials of legal liaison volunteers].

For the next half an hour police in riot formations charged the crowd forcing it down Brixton Hill. In the side streets many demonstrators (including myself) were caught between lines of riot police. We were ordered one way, and then ordered back as we reached the next line of police. Gradually, the crowd was forced down towards the tube station at the bottom of the hill. Hundreds of people were milling around watching what was happening. I watched with a friend:

We walked down to Electric Avenue. The market stalls were still lying around. People

dragged them into the middle of the road,
throwing cardboard boxes and other
rubbish on top. Then they were lit, more
were dragged up, a burning barricade
began to be formed. Then the riot police
again. It was unclear where to go. The
police were too close for us to run. They
charged. I grabbed Susan and threw her up
against the wall, covering our heads with
my arm. The riot police ran past us,
truncheoning down anyone in their path.
Danny Burns, extract from diary, 20/10/90.

We were lucky. Others were badly injured.
Over 40 police officers were wounded and, as
usual, it was impossible to tell how many civil-
ians were seriously hurt. 135 people were arrested, their charges ranged from Obstruction
to Riot. 27 people were charged with Violent
Disorder, an offence which carries a sentence of
up to five years.

This riot was not as significant as that of
Trafalgar Square. But the way it was docu-
mented provides some important political lessons. As a result of a highly planned approach
to defence, the TSDC was able to record minute
by minute everything that happened. This
meant that we could go onto the political offensive, and instead of *asserting* that the march had
been attacked by the police, this time we could
prove it.

A Planned Approach To Defence

The likelihood that the march to Brixton Prison
would be attacked made it extremely important that effective support work was done be-
forehand. The TSDC ensured that detailed
briefings were carried out. Stewards were sent
information about what they were expected to
do weeks in advance. 20,000 bust cards, out-
lining people's legal rights and giving a legal
contact number, were produced, and distributed on the demonstration. The TSDC sent
down its own video crew, which was trained to
take pictures which would not incriminate defendants. 60 legal liaison volunteers (LLVs)

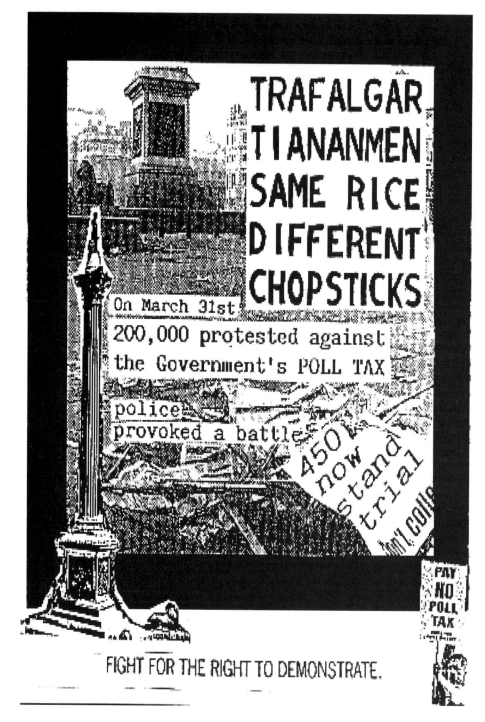

were on site wearing highly visible pink vests. They carried two-way radios (linked to a 48-hour co-ordination centre) and were, consequently, in a position to call up extra support wherever it was needed. They recorded all arrests, and got names and numbers of witnesses as they were happening. As I have mentioned over 135 people were arrested, 120 were charged. That evening volunteers were sent to every police station to welcome those who were released on bail.

This high degree of organisation produced results. This time every single one of the defendants had made direct contact with the campaign within the first week. A meeting was held the day after the demonstration which was attended by nearly 60 defendants. The legal liaison volunteers were brought together after the demonstration to collate their information and witness statements. Within twelve hours the campaign had a complete record of what had happened throughout the day. When they organised a press conference the next day:

The press thought that we would be a rabble, but they were stunned, they were surprised that we had the numbers of policemen who had said certain things; we had a complete chronology of events; and we were able to prove conclusively that the police had pre-planned attack.
Dave Morris, 25/4/91

The following day the media carried two versions of events, contrasting strongly with March 31st, when most newspapers carried only the views of the police and the political establishment.

At the beginning of 1991, the campaign realised that there was an increasing need to focus on prison support work. Up to then, solidarity work had been done outside the prisons, pickets had been organised etc., but no-one had thought much about what they could do for people inside. In January 1991, a prisoners support group was set up. By April it was supporting 27 long-term prisoners. This involved finding out the views of the prisoners; seeing if they wanted support and publicising their details to the Anti-Poll Tax movement. It also meant offering practical support. The TSDC made sure each prisoner was written to at least once a week by members of the campaign and visits to prisoners were co-ordinated through the campaign. Those who had been inside offered support and advice to those who were about to be convicted, and a newsletter was produced which published the letters of prisoners. The campaign needed a minimum of £1,000 per month just to provide basic welfare support to the prisoners. This paid for newspapers and books; a Walkman cassette player for every prisoner; £10 a month income (the maximum they are allowed). In addition to this some of the families were offered limited financial support for visits etc. Supporters of the campaign believed that those who were imprisoned were in prison on behalf of those who were outside, and it was the responsibility of the movement to take care of them. Some would still be inside in three or four years' time, and there still had to be an organisation there to support them.

The organisation which the Trafalgar Square Defendants' Campaign mobilised is a good model for future resistance movements . It made crystal clear that it is no good providing tokenistic support. It is the responsibility of any political movement to defend those who have fought for it. But this defence work can also have a political impact. If the campaign is well prepared and has accurate information it can go on to the political offensive and this will be vital to its success.

5

SINKING THE
FLAGSHIP

The aim of the Anti-Poll Tax campaign was to make the tax unworkable. If enough people refused to pay, then the Poll Tax couldn't be enforced. The courts would be blocked; the bailiffs would be turned away; wage arrestment would prove too complicated; and the final solution – prison – would prove politically disastrous for any Labour council (and in any case was unenforceable because there was no room for large numbers of non-payers in the prisons). The councils tried all of these enforcement measures but were persistently resisted by the Anti-Poll Tax Unions.

Councils In Chaos

Even before the campaign of resistance got underway, it received a massive helping hand from the councils who presided over the biggest administrative farce in British taxation history. For months it looked as if they were unlikely even to get the system up and running. The press was inundated with stories of bills which had been sent to babies and dead people. Councils were lambasted for their callousness and inefficiency.

At the heart of the problem was the Poll Tax register which had to be kept accurate and up to date. People were charged according to the length of time they had lived in the area, but in many areas, the population was changing so rapidly, it was impossible for the councils to keep up. A 1991 report by the Audit Commission showed that the register turnover was much higher than expected. Inner London had the worst figures with over 55% of the population changing address within the financial year. Even the shire district councils had a population turnover of 36% and, in the first year, Scottish local authorities had to make 1.5 million changes to the Poll Tax register.

In addition to this, councils were inundated with correspondence. Many people genuinely

Opposite: Timetabling the

enforcement process in

Scotland

128

didn't understand what the Poll Tax was about. Others mounted campaigns to delay registration by endlessly asking questions about the form. All of these had to be answered. Councils sat under a mountain of paper. Everything they did seemed to create more work:

> The paper-work involved with administering the charge is enormous – and likely to get worse. Backlogs switch from one area of activity to another. Indeed, local authorities cannot really do anything without generating more paper-work. If they attempt to canvas more people for registration they will also produce more people who will refuse to register.
>
> Poll Tax Legal Group, Law Review No.4, March 1991.

The problems didn't stop there. Councils which were capped had to send out new bills which doubled their work load. Then people wrote in to say that they didn't understand which bill they were supposed to have paid. The cycle of administrative chaos got worse with each day. In May, Bristol's *Venue* magazine reported:

> There is no immediate prospect of reminders being sent out to those who haven't paid. The council's Poll Tax officers are too busy trying to sort out a variety of disasters and administrative nightmares including:
>
> • The half built Poll Tax HQ, Amelia Court – It had been hoped that work would have finished on the building before the bills were sent out. Last month the construction firm went into liquidation.
> • Poll Tax payment books which few people have received. The machine being used to print them broke down.
> • A predicted 25% change in the Poll Tax register over the coming year.
>
> Venue, 1/5/90.

In Lothian, it was widely reported that

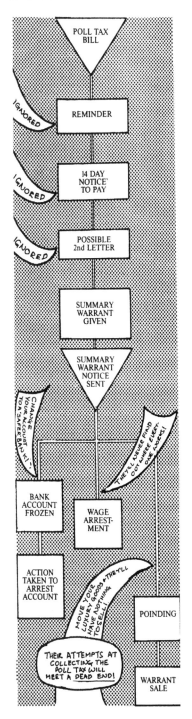

Anti-Poll Tax activists had managed to put a bug into the computer, which randomly wiped out every sixth record on the register. The virus story was never proven. However, a month before it was mentioned in the newspapers, its effects were accurately described to two Anti-Poll Tax activists by two computer hackers one of whom had worked for Lothian Regional Council and had been sacked.

Wherever the council registration officers went they were harassed. In Glasgow violent threats drove canvasser Robert Stevenson to quit his job. He was physically threatened twice in four weeks and continually harassed:

I'd just put the form through the door when this guy across in the garden opposite started shouting. He was sitting in the garden with about four others and they were all giving me dirty looks. He said that if I came back to collect the form I would need a tank for protection. I was in no doubt that they were serious. I didn't finish my last street. I just chucked it.
Glasgow Evening Times, 9/7/88.

The Evening Times reported the case of another canvasser who was 'harassed by a gang'. In this case, it was reported that:

Four or five youths cornered him in a close in Gairbraid Avenue and subjected him to abuse. A Strathclyde police spokesman revealed: 'They said it was a 'No Poll Tax Area' and told the worker to get out, which he did.'

Following these reports, the Poll Tax registration officer admitted that 'there had been at least four other incidents involving canvassers' and that his work-force had found letter-boxes blocked by campaigners, barbed-wire wrapped around garden gates and canvassers had been threatened (leaflets were grabbed from their hands). Already over two members of his staff had resigned because of fears about their personal safety. This general level of har-

Opposite: A defiant

warning from local

activists.

130

assment badly affected morale. Some such as Mr. Trueman, a Poll Tax snooper whose job was to call on people and badger them into filling the registration forms, were unable to cope with the abuse that they received:

Mrs. Trueman found the corpse of her husband as she came back from shopping. Fred Trueman, 52, an employee of Bristol City, had hanged himself. 'No-one can imagine what terrible pressure he had to work under,' she claimed. 'He was sworn at and threatened; he couldn't stand it any more'
Der Spiegel, 5/3/90.

But it was not only the canvassers who were at risk. As well as these individual cases of harassment, there were incidents which led to fears for office staff safety. In Cambridgeshire two petrol bombs were thrown at the Poll Tax Headquarters and Anti-Poll Tax slogans were sprayed on the side of the building (only one of the petrol bombs ignited and no-one was injured).

These events aren't only important because of what they say about the morale of the Poll Tax office workers. They also tell us something about the degree of anger about the tax. Ordinary people on local estates were expressing what they felt. Sometimes this manifested itself as intimidation, occasionally as physical violence, but it was real anger. It was not orchestrated by any political group. This gave it a greater impact.

Council Poll Tax departments began to face a major recruitment crisis. Despite the fact that they were offering higher salaries and part-time rates to Poll Tax staff, few wanted to work there. Many were simply outraged by the Poll Tax and would not work for it on moral grounds. Others were aware of the very real consequences – of losing friends and constant abuse:

Of 210 full-time workers, it has only managed to recruit 145 so far, whereas the

[Anti-Poll Tax] federation is inundated with
volunteers who manage to fit in one
morning, afternoon or evening shift between jobs and family commitments
Bristol Evening Post, 9/5/90.

Even before the impact of non-payment,
councils were struggling to keep their heads
above water, but morale in the Anti-Poll Tax
Unions was high.

Taking The Battle Into The Courts

We will clog the courts with non-payers, we
will make them unworkable. The Anti-Poll
Tax Unions will support the people in their
fight for basic rights, and when the people
turn up in their hundreds and thousands
the Poll Tax will be made unenforceable.
Danny Burns, speech to Bristol demonstration, March 1990.

It was after lunch. A fraction of the 1,845
cases had been processed; delaying tactics
were working, some reaching the level of
stand up comedy, others that of surreal
farce... A heckler was dragged out by police
– the court became jittery, Mr. Rice cleared
the public gallery, then it was Michael
Harrison's turn. Single-handedly he reduced the day to the fiasco it had been
warming up to – his determined questions
about why reminders were sent out second
class paid off. All summonses withdrawn,
£8,000 down the drain.
*Description of the Medina Council court cases, Local Govern-
ment Chronicle, 15/6/90.*

By the middle of 1990, official figures showed
that millions of people hadn't paid the Poll Tax.
These people would all have to be taken to

court. In England and Wales, councils had to get a court 'liability order' for each non-payer before they were allowed to proceed with action to recover the Poll Tax. Councils had gone through a similar process to recover debts under the rates and generally saw it as a formality. However, the sheer numbers involved in non-payment of the Poll Tax made this situation quite different. Bristol City Council issued summonses to 120,000 people, Leeds summoned 110,000 and the numbers in almost all other big cities were comparable. In order to get through this number of cases, councils had to hope that defendants wouldn't turn up. Courts are busy places, they often have little time available to listen to civil cases of this nature, and in many areas councils could not expect to be allocated more than ten or twenty days of court time in a year.

The strategy of the Anti-Poll Tax Unions was to make sure that as many people as possible came to court. In law everyone had a right to have their case heard individually. The calculation was that even if only a small percentage of people had their cases heard, the courts would be blocked for years.

Initially, neither the councils nor the courts took the judicial procedure seriously because they didn't expect anyone to turn up. They had never done so under the rates, so they had no reason to believe that they would do now. Medina Council (on the Isle of Wight) summoned 3,000 people to attend court on a single day. South Tyneside Council summoned 3,500 to appear on two afternoons. A total of five hours was allocated to hear all these cases – an average of four seconds per hearing. When people heard this they were furious, because it was obvious that both the council and the courts saw the process as a rubber stamping exercise. Many people had assumed that if they couldn't pay then they could go to court and explain their situation. This was obviously not going to be the case.

The Anti-Poll Tax Unions publicised the strategy to block the courts, with leaflets and posters and articles in the local newspapers.

Mass demonstrations were called for the first day of the hearings, and in some areas the courts were brought to a standstill. In Warrington on June 28th 1990, 1,000 people took over the court and all the cases were postponed. Similar events took place in Southwark:

> 1,500 people, mostly women and children, turned up at Southwark court and occupied the building. It was absolute chaos, the courts couldn't handle the numbers. The police were stopping people from coming into their own court cases. The crowd didn't move until the court declared all 5,000 cases adjourned.
> *Counter Information, No.30, February 1991.*

In every part of England and Wales local groups mobilised to provide support for non-payers in the courts. Tens, if not hundreds of activists in each region attended legal briefing sessions. These were run both by activists and sympathetic local lawyers. People were given ideas about how they might disrupt or delay the court proceedings. These included simple things, like asking for a glass of water because their throat was dry, demanding to see the identity cards of everyone present in court, to fainting in court or arranging for fire alarms to go off. People were told to demand their rights to see and read every document which was produced as evidence against them. They were also given briefings on the basic technical arguments.

By October 1990, when most of the court cases had started, virtually every Anti-Poll Tax Union in the UK had trained at least two or three of its members to become conversant with the Poll Tax law. Throughout England and Wales over a thousand people were trained to do court support work and could quote the relevant legislation. This is unique in the history of popular campaigning. The Anti-Poll Tax Unions hoped to use the legal precedent of McKenzie versus McKenzie (1970), which said that a person can 'attend a trial as a

135

friend of either party (to) take notes and quietly make suggestions and give advice to that party'. This person would be known as a 'McKenzie friend'. McKenzie friends had no right to address the court, but they could advise the non-payer what to say. In this way everyone would be able to offer technical defences and thereby delay the proceedings.

The campaign needed lawyers only in the most technical cases. Lawyers were often seen as a liability, because they represented an individual client, and it was in their interest to get through the procedure as quickly as possible. It was in the campaign's interest for everything to proceed as slowly as possible. Nevertheless, legal knowledge and guidance was essential. This arrived with the creation of the Poll Tax Legal Group, an organisation which was set up by two Anti-Poll Tax activists from Hackney: Alan Murdie and Len Lucas. The Poll Tax Legal Group researched legislation and case law. It set up a network of lawyers throughout England and Wales who could support the legal challenges of Anti-Poll Tax groups and produced over 30 accessible legal bulletins on the Poll Tax and a book called *To Pay or Not To Pay*. These underpinned the legal needs of the movement and helped ordinary people to get to grips with the law they needed to use.

Many magistrates immediately restricted the use of McKenzie friends, arguing that they had discretion over when and where it was appropriate to allow them. They often adopted very questionable criteria. In Bristol, people were asked their profession. They were allowed a McKenzie friend if they were a building worker and not if they were a teacher. Presumably, they assumed that manual workers were thick, and teachers intelligent. The hypocrisy of the courts was exposed by their sheer irrationality. The following exchange summed up the situation:

Magistrate: You are a teacher, you have read the liability order and understand what is written on it, so why do you need a friend?

Non-payer: Because this is a complicated matter of law and I have never had any dealings with the law.

Magistrate: Well, I'm sure you are quite capable of understanding the proceedings without help. They should be quite straight forward for someone with your background

Non-payer: Well, if they're so simple why do you have to keep asking the learned clerk what to do every five minutes? You obviously don't understand it yourself.

A legal challenge by the Leicester Rights Centre in the High Court, ruled that magistrates were under no obligation to allow McKenzie friends. This judgement was later overruled by the appeal court in July 1991, but by this stage the McKenzie friend strategy was not proving too successful anyway, mainly because non-payers had little time before their

A typical court scene. The chair of the magistrates sits under the coat of arms, flanked by two other magistrates. In front of him is the clerk of the court. In the foreground the court usher stands in a dark cloak, and to the right, a non-payer stands with her McKenzie friend.

court cases to become familiar with the technical arguments their McKenzie friends were trying to convey. Nevertheless, the campaign managed to reduce the speed of Poll Tax cases to a slow crawl.

This was possible because activists shifted their tactics towards giving detailed briefings outside the courts and focusing on the most common areas on which the councils had been wrong-footed (for example, getting addresses wrong and not giving enough notice). Non-payers were also advised to prepare a political speech and not to stop talking (so that they couldn't be interrupted by the magistrate). Experience showed that the most effective way of wasting time, for those who were not familiar with the law, was to relate direct experiences of hardship. People talking in their own language about their own circumstances were much harder for the magistrates to dismiss than legal technicians. Many people made political speeches which lasted for as long as ten minutes, others outlined their financial circum-

Bristol non-payers wait apprehensively for their court cases.

Mark Simmons

Dear Chris,

I'm sorry this is being written with such a delayed time factor, but the little people here at home make insatiable demands on my time, it's just a brief note to thank you very much for your support and help as my "Mckenzie Friend," on that nervewracking day of 30th July in the Bath Magistrates Court. Before I met you I must admit I had started to let the situation overwhelm me, very early that morning I had left behind me a very worried husband (trying not to show it) and four apprehensive children, (Oliver was looking forward to the bus rides!) three of whom saw the prospect of Mum in Prison as a realised nightmare.

I had declined the company of a very good friend, because of the very early start, cost of fare and the misguided belief I could handle it, I say misguided as after I had left the court I wandered towards Bath shopping centre, to find myself sitting on a bench before a church in tears, with a very puzzled Oliver watching me from his pushchair.

Thank you again, especially as you and your companions have reinforced my faith in humankind, in that you helped and supported me, a stranger in a vunerable situation.

Yours sincerely.

Jo

stances. They all took up valuable time, and sometimes made a powerful and moving impact on the public gallery.

The detailed briefings held outside the court-room were combined with political speeches from activists about the campaign. This political presence was an important confidence booster for those who were being processed through the court system. They saw how professionally the campaign was organised and this strengthened their resolve not to pay.

Few of those turning up to court had had any previous contact with their local Anti-Poll Tax Union, so the court waiting-rooms provided a place in which people could meet other non-payers from their local area. It was often their first opportunity to organise together, and as a result, a number of new Anti-Poll Tax Unions were formed in the waiting rooms. Using the time constructively in this way helped to keep people interested, and ensured that people stayed at the courts all day.

In some areas, the scale of the operation in the courts was immense. In Bristol the campaign had five activists available two days a week solely for court support work. Briefings were delivered every ten minutes or so for the first two hours each day and a creche was organised. In Bristol, where over 10% of non-payers consistently turned up to court over a period of five months, there were always willing volunteers. But this experience was not universal. In most rural areas, local groups found it hard to sustain any presence at all after the first week. Even cities like Leeds found it fairly difficult to persuade non-payers to turn up to court. Other activists had similar experiences:

Some activists in Stamford Hill Anti-Poll Tax Union felt that the massive emphasis on court work could lead the movement up a blind alley. It was very difficult to inspire people in court. Most people went in desperation, and left the court even more desperate and frightened.
Alan Hirons, Stamford Hill APTU, 3/9/91.

140

Nevertheless, in most courts the public galleries were full. People were learning how the courts worked, some awed by the situation, others amused by the ridiculousness of the pomp and ceremony. Extremely technical cases were punctuated by pure farce. Some examples of exchanges between magistrates and non-payers indicate how easy it was to ridicule the courts :

Court clerk: Are you Mr. I. Smith?
Non-payer: No, I am Mr. I. T. Smith.
Court clerk: Mr. Smith, you did respond to a notice to come to this court which was addressed to Mr. I. Smith did you not?
Non-payer: Yes.
Court clerk: Then are you not Mr. I. Smith?
Non-payer: No, I'm Mr. I. T. Smith
Court clerk: Well, if you aren't Mr. I. Smith then why did you answer the summons?
Non-payer: Because I wanted to make sure you didn't mistake me for Mr. I. Smith.
Court clerk: Mr. Smith, is there anyone else in your house who might be called Mr. I. Smith?
Non-payer: I don't know
Court clerk: Do you live with your family?
Non-payer: No
Court clerk: Well, what sort of house do you live in?
Non-payer: An ordinary terraced house.
Court clerk: Do you own the house Mr. Smith?
Non-payer: Yes.
Court clerk: Well, does anyone else live there?
Non-payer: I'm not sure, there might be someone living in the spare room.
Court clerk: You don't know who lives in your spare room?
Non-payer: No.
Court Clerk: Mr. Smith are you sure that you haven't got anyone living under the floorboards of your house?

(The names in this dialogue have been changed.)

Exchanges of this sort were meaningless, and

didn't constitute any sort of defence, but this was the essence of the strategy.

People also made use of their personal circumstances and played them to their limits:

There was a chap from Pudsey. He told me that he was a diabetic and that he might need to give himself some Insulin. So he dragged his court-case on as long as possible. It was about fifteen minutes, then he shuddered and explained to the magistrate that he needed his jab, and asked if it was OK if he gave it to himself. They said fine and he rolled up his T-shirt in full view of them and stuck a needle into his stomach. One of the magistrates looked as if she was going to be sick.

Ian Greaves, Secretary, Leeds Federation APTUs,11/5/91.

These exchanges got a good deal of local media publicity and demoralised the court officials. While they soon became adept at minimising this sort of wilful disruption, they never eradicated it.

Some extremely interesting legal defences were mounted. One was a claim that if you were a Cornish tin miner you were exempt from the Poll Tax. A Cornish tin miner was technically someone who held shares in a Cornish tin mine and the Stannary Parliament of Cornwall:

The argument was that by virtue of a Royal Charter of 1508, the Stannary Parliament has a power of veto over all taxes levied by the government on tin miners, descendants of tin miners in perpetuity, owners of tin mines and workers in the tin industry.

Poll Tax Legal Group, 1990.

This was made possible because, in 1974, a Cornishman Fred Trull revived the Cornish Stannary Parliament and became its clerk. Fred Trull started selling shares which cost £1 plus 50p for postage and packing. The press liked the story and covered it extensively. As a result,

West Hampstead Anti Poll Tax Union

TO ALL POLL TAX NON-PAYERS WHO RECEIVE A SUMMONS

TURN UP IN COURT

......and tire the magistrate

DEMONSTRATE FROM FRI.9th. NOV.1pm.
NEXT COURT CASES
HAMPSTEAD MAGISTRATES COURT, DOWNSHIRE HILL N.W.3.

Leon Kuhn

Fred Trull, started to receive thousands of letters; on one day he received over 100,000 letters of application for shares. He had to hire a local hall and enlist two dozen volunteers to deal with the mail. He said:

> Legally they can do nothing about it. On what pretext can a foreign government take a foreign national to their courts.

Unfortunately they did do something about it. Fred Trull was arrested for illegally selling shares, and his legal argument, after trundling through the High Court for some time, finally ground to a halt. Nevertheless, he had provided people with something else to argue about in court.

Delaying tactics were mixed with serious legal technicalities. Councils were challenged, for sending notices to the wrong addresses. Given the rate at which people moved houses, it was difficult for the councils to keep up, and as a result many cases were dropped because people hadn't received proper notice. Big legal challenges were also made over 'correct procedures'. These came in the first few weeks and resulted mostly from the inexperience of councils in dealing with this sort of process. The first day of Medina Council's cases (on the Isle of Wight) is probably the most famous example. The reminder notices were sent out with second class stamps, they consequently arrived late, people didn't receive the statutory notice which they were entitled to, and the court threw out all 1,900 cases. The council had to start again.

Leon Kuhn

143

Justice Is Not Seen To Be Done!

'Now for the evidence,' said the King, 'and then the sentence.'
'No!' said the Queen, 'First the sentence and then the evidence.'
'Nonsense!' cried Alice, 'The idea of having the sentence first.'
Lewis Caroll, Alice Through The Looking Glass., 1872

One of the unique factors about the Poll Tax court cases was that magistrates were not allowed to take into account the circumstances of the people who were up before them. This was written into the legislation and marked a complete departure from the rates system. In rates cases magistrates had the power to waive debts if they believed defendants were suffering genuine hardship. Under the Poll Tax, magistrates could only take people's financial circumstances into account when the local authority had tried every other means of recovering the money and the non-payer was in court again facing imprisonment. This infuriated people, because they came to the courts in their hundreds, armed with figures about how much they spent on food, how much on clothes, how much on rent and how much was left. They believed that if they could prove that they literally had no money then the courts would show them justice. Unfortunately, it was not that simple:

We aren't here to discuss political issues...
We aren't here to decide whether you can afford to pay or not...
Local Government Chronicle, 15/6/90.

These same lines were repeated in court after court. Frequently magistrates would talk over the non-payers while they were in the middle of a sentence: 'liability order granted, fine £18.50, next case please.' The magistrates then signalled to the police officer and the non-payers were hustled out of the court, protesting that they hadn't finished their defence. Often people didn't realise the case was over because they were still in the middle of speaking when the magistrates pronounced 'guilt'.

One woman in a Bristol court brought in a detailed list of all her income and living costs. These showed that after she had paid for basic necessities, she only had £3.50 a week left (Poll Tax for her and her husband amounted to nearly £20 per week). After she had explained this to the magistrate, the clerk of the court replied dryly, 'Is that the only reason why you have not paid your Poll Tax?' This disregard of basic circumstances contravened most peoples' understanding of justice. While it is true that technically the courts didn't have any discretion to consider circumstances, they did have the power to treat people with dignity and listen to what they had to say.

In some areas, anyone who started to put a serious case forward, had their case stopped in the middle, and were told that if they wanted to be heard they would have to wait until the end of the day. It seemed farcical that people were being punished for presenting a case when they thought that this was what the courts were there for. For many, this was their first experience of the British judicial system, an institution some had respected in the past. Their respect soon turned to rage:

> They didn't listen to a word I said... They just made an order while I was talking, there isn't any justice in the courts, but I didn't expect justice because it's impossible to administer this tax in a just way.

> I'm appalled at the way the magistrates abused people psychologically, they were very intimidating.

> Its' just disgraceful intimidation of the population, people are being hassled through, not being allowed to say anything or make a case even if they have a case... people aren't being allowed to have any support whatsoever. It seems really strange in this day and age that this is allowed to happen.

This is a kangaroo court, they aren't allowing people to have a proper defence, the
magistrates are making this a political trial.

*Interviews with people after they had appeared in court, Bristol
Magistrates Court, 1/2/91.*

Despite this, the court strategy was effective in delaying the granting of liability orders.
Some courts, like Hackney in London, were
severely disabled. Others, like Bristol, slogged
their way through the cases but, as I have
described, were still hopelessly far from their
targets. In Bristol, where the magistrates were
stricter than in most areas, 1,600 people were
summoned every Friday. Unfortunately for the
council, well over 150 non-payers came to have
their cases heard each week. On some weeks,
where there were strong Anti-Poll Tax Unions
(they summoned people on an area basis) 400-
500 people turned up. Over a period of five
months, over 10% of those summoned consistently arrived at the courts to have their cases
heard. The mathematics were simple. Even if
cases only averaged five minutes each (and
some took considerably longer), with an average of 10% of those summoned turning up, the
courts would need 120 full days of court time
(they were only able to negotiate about 35 from
a busy court before the end of the financial
year) to get liability orders for the 120,000 non-
payers. By the end of the first financial year of
the Poll Tax they had got less than half.

Many councils tried using the press to dis-
suade people from turning up. Local papers,
such as the *Docklands Recorder* in Tower Hamlets, printed long lists of non-payers in an attempt to shame them in public. This plan failed
miserably as hundreds of people wrote to the
letters' pages asking why they weren't on the
list, saying they were proud to be non-payers
and wanted everyone to know. The lists also
gave a helping hand to campaigners who were
finding it hard to get hold of information on
who had been through the courts, because the
councils and the courts had refused to make the
lists public. Now the activists were able to look

them up in the newspaper. This information was vital for the next stage – telling people personally about their rights in relation to bailiffs and wage arrestment.

This extraordinarily successful campaign in the courts was only the beginning of the enforcement nightmare for the local councils. In many areas, it would take years just to get the pieces of paper to allow them to start enforcement action. Actually getting the money would be another story!

No Bailiffs Here!

There can be no greater infringement of an individual's civil liberties than to have a sheriff officer examine their personal belongings to ascertain if there is anything worth poinding

David Begg – Chair of Finance, Lothian Regional Council, Local Government Chronicle, 14/9/90.

Bailiffs are legally sanctioned thugs who are employed to recover debts from people who have not got the money to pay them. In the fight against non-payment, bailiffs and Scottish sheriff officers were used indiscriminately by councils to harass and degrade the poor. In England and Wales, they were authorised by law to take furniture and household goods from those people who had no other assets (in Scotland they could only take 'luxury' goods). This procedure is called 'distraint'. In 1986, the Law Commission recommended the abolition of distraint. That recommendation was ignored.

Labour councils were just as thorough in their use of bailiffs as Tory ones. This is all the more remarkable as, even in pure economic terms, the cost of recovery was likely to be far higher than what was raised. Poor people don't tend to own much, and the resale value of what they do own is likely to be minimal – certainly

147

not enough to pay the £400 or £500 Poll Tax demanded by many councils. Most people will do anything they can to pay a debt, before allowing the bailiffs to come in and sell off everything they own at a fraction of what it is worth. So, it is only the very poorest who have no alternative source of money who will allow themselves to reach the stage of bailiff action. For many the only way of paying the debt was to go to the loan sharks, and it is clear that the establishment was well-aware of this:

Remember household goods don't produce large prices at auction and replacement of those goods on credit can make the situation worse.
Local Government Chronicle, supplement 16, November 1990.

But most councils seemed less concerned about the actual impact of these actions than the way they were perceived. One piece of advice from the *Local Government Chronicle* was: 'The word bailiff is an emotive one, and gentler titles should be used.' But no amount of cosmetic dressing could disguise the naked brutality of the bailiffs' work. In Scotland the process of distraint was particularly degrading. Sheriff officers had the right to recover debts without a full court hearing. They would send round threatening letters in an attempt to intimidate people into paying. If this failed they turned up on the doorstep to carry out a 'poinding' – a valuation of people's goods. To do this they had to get into people's houses and, in Scotland (if they gave four days' notice), they had the right to break and enter. The sheriff officers then had the right to hold 'warrant sales' (public auctions of people's goods) inviting the public to buy the goods for a pittance. Debtors didn't only have to suffer the loss of their few personal possessions but also to face the humiliation of exposing their desperate financial plight to their friends and neighbours.

In England and Wales, the situation was not quite so bad. Bailiffs could only be used after liability orders had been granted in the courts. Bailiffs didn't have the right to force

149

entry. They were allowed to climb through an open window, and if, unknowingly, the non-payer let the bailiff into their house the first time, the bailiff subsequently had the right to break in. But, if they were consistently stopped at the door, they had no right to enter, however many times they came back:

> Their powers of entry are rather like those traditionally associated with vampires – they have to be invited in or allowed in by an occupant of the property, or find an open door or window.
> *Poll Tax Legal Group, 1990.*

These differences between Scotland and the rest of the UK compelled the Anti-Poll Tax Unions to adopt different strategies. In Scotland, the focus was on getting hundreds of people outside homes which were threatened, and physically stopping the bailiffs. This particular battle was more intense because it was the last course of action the councils could take – people couldn't be imprisoned for debt in Scotland. In England and Wales, while organising physical defence against the bailiffs was important, the main focus was on huge propaganda campaigns to make sure that people knew their rights.

In most cases of debt, before the Poll Tax was introduced, just the threat of the bailiffs was enough to secure payment. According to Simon Smith, the Secretary of the Association of Certified Bailiffs for England and Wales:

> Under the rates, goods were actually removed in only around 1% of cases – 99% of the time the bailiffs secured payment or the promise of payment.
> *Labour Research, October 1990.*

> Normally when goods are poinded, the debtors see how low a value the sheriff officers are placing on their goods and somehow find the money, often by borrowing from relatives, to pay up.
> *Glasgow Herald, 1/7/89.*

Because of this, distraint was seen by councils as an efficient method of debt collection. The situation had got so bad in the past because few people knew their rights. So, when bailiffs had intimidated people into letting them in, or barged the door down, often with police collusion, there was no community resistance.

So the first task of Anti-Poll Tax Unions was to inform people about what the bailiffs could and couldn't do. In Scotland, people were advised not to tell the sheriffs where they worked, not to tell them which banks they used and not, under any circumstances, to let them into their houses. They were also told to inform the local group as soon as the sheriffs threatened anything. The Anti-Poll Tax Unions advised people to move possessions to local friends' houses before the date of the poinding and offered to help with the moving. People were told to leave their cars well away from their homes. They were informed that a wrongful poinding could be appealed against and, in many cases, this was done successfully. People were also told how to avoid bailiff action by signing away their possessions to people who lived outside of the area or, preferably, to their children. There are now young children who technically own all of their parents' possessions.

Some local law centres went onto the offensive against the bailiffs, providing information to the public, which totally undermined their actions. One morning in May 1991, the bailiffs delivered over 4,000 intimidation notices to people throughout Bristol. By 7.30 am. the law centre had heard about this and contacted all local radio stations. By 8.00 p.m. the news bulletins which went out every fifteen minutes, reported:

Today bailiffs have delivered notices for payment to over 4,000 people in Bristol. A spokesperson from the law centre said that they were illegal and should be ignored.

So most people ignored them. This is a good example of the way in which voluntary groups were able to contribute to the campaign.

BEAT THE BAILIFFS!

DON'T PANIC DON'T PAY!

- A bailiff is only allowed to enter your home if you have let them in.
- If you do let them in they can use force on later visits.
- Council officials may well be doing the bailiffs job at first.
- Bailiffs can enter through an open window, so keep them locked.
- Tell your children not to open the door.
- Ask a friend to be a witness to prevent illegal action, better still contact your local anti-poll tax group.

Join the Bailiff Busters

255 - 504

While an important part of the resistance to the bailiffs, propaganda was not enough. Direct responses needed to be organised. Action against the bailiffs was planned months in advance. Throughout Britain, city-wide bailiff busting groups were formed. Activists in Edinburgh formed a group called 'Scum-busters' which was equipped with CB radios, and squadrons of cars. Telephone trees were organised; bailiff companies were monitored; their car registration numbers were taken and distributed to activists in all the local areas. Camden, in London, followed their example in 1991:

152

We have organised a rota so that we know who and when people are available to do whatever shift. We have organised a 'knock up system' giving people different responsibilities for knocking up each part of the estate when the bailiffs are spotted. Telephone trees have also been established. We have approached a couple of mini-cab firms who have agreed to be bailiff spotters... We visited the bailiff's office in Wandsworth and, believe me, they are worried. After all they are used to intimidating old-aged pensioners and one parent families but now they know we are organised it's a different story.

Josie Alverez, Mornington Crescent APTU, Camden, London, All-Britain Anti-Poll Tax Federation newsletter, September 1990.

In Bristol a bailiff monitoring group was formed. The bailiffs Roach and Co. were permanently watched for a week; their vehicle details were taken. Information was found out about individual bailiffs; their home addresses were distributed to the local groups. Pickets were regularly organised outside their offices.

The first Scottish people to face poindings were given advance warning by the sheriff officers. This gave them the legal power to force entry, but also enabled the Anti-Poll Tax Unions to prepare for their arrival. The sheriffs' first attempt was at the Glasgow home of Jeannette McGuin on Tuesday July 4th 1989. Jeannette owed just £59 for non-registration. Over 300 people turned up outside her house. Banners were hung out of the window saying 'God Help the Sheriffs'. The sheriffs didn't show up and Jeannette McGuin never heard another word from them. As the non-payment cases began to emerge, the level of activity picked up. For example, in Edinburgh over 300 people filled a central high street to prevent a poinding on March 3rd. 200 activists guarded flats in the Grass Market area on April 11th, and 150 people guarded 11 flats in Stockbridge and Comely Bank on April 17th and 18th – an event which featured two street parties, a march around the local area, and the physical chasing of two sheriff officers out of the area. Similar situations developed across Scotland:

The very first poinding which was supposed to have been taking place was in a small village called Pathead. The woman was getting a bit worried, she'd had no contact whatsoever with any Anti-Poll Tax groups, but she'd heard about the Anti-Poll Tax movement. She'd phoned up the federation office. The federation phoned me as a contact... I spoke to her, telling her I could get her help in the area if she wanted the people to come. She was a bit dubious to start with. She thought, 'Oh well, he's only saying that, the Anti-Poll Tax movement willn'y come and help me. I mean Pathead must have been fifteen to sixteen miles from Edinburgh, would people come from that area for to help us.' So I went up again on the Thursday, explained everything again to her, reassured her...

I put up the Mayfield/Newtongrange banner in her garden, took along the federation banner, hung that from her window... The back of eight o'clock everybody started coming up, they actually started running a relay service, a shuttle service with cars going to collect people, and I'd say by about half-past nine to ten o'clock we had 110 people standing in the garden. It was a beautiful day, it was like everybody was sunbathing, having a day out, we stood about there, everybody singing songs, we had the records on, a couple of them had a wee drink, things like that, waiting on the sheriff officers coming... So she thought 'I wonder if the Anti-Poll Tax movement is going to stay here because they had a lot of poindings on that day?' But I guaranteed her we'd have people there from eight in the morning to eight at night.

The sheriff officers turned up, got on the phone and, lo and behold, a police car turned up... So the police came up and asked us if the sheriff officers could get in and I said 'Well, I'm telling you, under no circumstances whatsoever are we allowing any sheriff officers into anybody's house to carry out a poinding.'

So everyone was shouting and jeering in the garden and that, they were dancing about and that. I says to them, 'Listen, could you keep quiet just now so that we can hear what the police and the sheriff officers are saying?' So the sheriff officers turned around to the police, and says 'I want him arrested, because he's organising this,' and the police says 'Well, we can't do a thing.' And everyone in the garden, I says to them well, 'They want me arrested.' They says, 'Well, if you're getting arrested then all of us are getting arrested.' And by this time, the local coalman had come up the road in his lorry, stopped his lorry and blocked the street. The two guys at the back jumped off, and the coalman who was driving the lorry, they jumped over the fence and joined us. The local council workers, who were doing the windows at the time, downed their tools and got in the garden and supported us. It's worse than jungle drums, because the local baker heard it, he came around with his baker's van and started dishing out cakes to us. The sheriff officers were getting quite panicky by this time. The police got in their car and left the sheriff officers. I told them again. I said, 'You'd better get going, it's a waste of your time, we know you're not going to get in, so there's nothing else you can do.' So they asked for the woman in the house... She spoke to them over the gate. I says, 'The first thing that you must tell me – you're a sheriff officer?' He says, 'I am.' I says, 'Well, look, I want identification,' because they carry a card, and their photograph. So he had a big folder. He opened the folder, his hands were shaking that much that I had to have the folder and take his identification out for him. I got the identification, he showed her it and I says, 'Well, what's your business?' He says, 'Well,' he says to, Mabel Brown, her name was, 'We're here to execute this summary warrant on you for to gain entry into your house to carry out a poinding.' We took it off him. I says to Mabel, 'Well, you know what to do with that,' so she ripped it up, took it into the house and threw it in the fire. I says to them, 'There's no way you're getting in,' so they were quite persistent. They tried to get in for five or ten minutes and by this time the crowd were getting quite hostile, and I says, 'I think you'd better go to you're car while you've still got four wheels and you're still able to walk.'

Jackie Moyers, Mayfield/Newtongrange Anti-Poll Tax Union, 6/5/91.

In the South West of England the preparations for the bailiffs were put to the test on August 3rd 1990. Bailiffs from Roach and Co. (Bristol) were due to go both to Barry, near Cardiff, and the village of Bishops Lydeard near Taunton. A picket was called by the Avon Federation of Anti-Poll Tax Unions for 7.00 a.m. outside Roach's headquarters. This was aimed at getting maximum publicity across the day, and blockading any vehicles which happened to go from the central compound. At the same time federation members set up a watch on the Severn Bridge. At 7.30 a.m. one of Roach's cars was spotted crossing the bridge. This was telephoned through to the Cardiff Federation who had 50 people waiting on the estate which the bailiffs were due to visit. The car was later spotted three miles away with its tyres slashed. In the meantime over 100 people had been on the end of telephones waiting to be called up if necessary.

The action at Bishops Lydeard was even more dramatic. A large number of the tiny village's population took the day off work. They divided up into small groups, and blockaded every road into the village. Barricades were constructed and every vehicle which tried to enter was stopped and asked its business.

Mark Simmons

156

Cars were driven up and down the country lanes to spot the bailiffs. In the end, the bailiffs didn't come near the place.

In one or two places when the bailiffs got desperate, they made attempts to distrain goods found outside people's houses. A classic example came from Bristol when Roach and Co. attempted to get into the house of someone on their list for non-payment. They couldn't gain entry so they took away his garden equipment (including the lawn mower) and three cars which were parked outside his house. It didn't occur to them that if he were not paying the Poll Tax, he probably didn't have much money, so he probably didn't have three cars. The next day they discovered that one of the cars was owned by the next door neighbour, and the man from whom they had intended to seize goods had actually paid his Poll Tax. He sued for illegal distraint and joined the Anti-Poll Tax Union, saying that he was not going to pay next year.

But the campaign was not only defensive.

Families in Barry wait

outside their homes for the

bailiffs to arrive.

Mark Simmons

157

Many local activists decided to visit the bailiffs in *their* homes, and let them know that they were not welcome in our communities. On May 1st 1991, around 80 activists from around the South-West converged on the little town of Nempnett Thrubwell, where Mr. Roach the owner of the Bristol based bailiff company lived. This extract from my diary describes the event:

We thought Mr. Roach needed to see what it felt like to be intimidated in his home... The press were all there. Mr. Roach wasn't. We informed all his neighbours that Mr. Roach was a bailiff. 'Oh,' said one of them, 'I wondered why he had such a flash car.' Another, an old bloke, came out of his house wielding a stick. He said, 'You shouldn't interfere with other people's property.' 'That's what we've come to tell Mr. Roach,' we replied. At about 7.30 p.m. we saw the others come over the horizon with banners and slogans, filling the country lanes with chants of 'We won't pay the Poll Tax'. The village didn't really know what had hit it. There were certainly more Anti-Poll Tax activists than houses. Everyone gathered around Roach's house. A banner which read 'Bristol Bailiff Assassins' was planted on his lawn. It just so happened, that Mr. Roach had been building himself a garden wall and there were a lot of new bricks lying around, so people started to brick up his doors and windows. Others had a look at Mr. Roach's double garage – the door was open. Any good bailiff should know that if you want to keep your property safe, you shouldn't leave your door open. Well, there wasn't a car inside, but there was a mountain bike; fishing tackle, clothes, bottles of wine, garden equipment. In fact, the place was chock-a-block. A mock auction was held in front of the press. Anyway, his possessions ended up strewn all over the garden, and slogans were daubed across the back of his wall: 'Fuck off bailiff, we'll be back!' The police arrived

about five minutes after we had gone. We
heard that Mr. Roach was escorted home
later that night in a police car. It's good to
give people like that a taste of their own
medicine.
Danny Burns, extract from diary, 2/5/91.

The story, which was widely covered by the
regional press, made people laugh and made
the point that they didn't have to wait help-
lessly until the bailiffs came to them. It also
inspired other actions elsewhere. In Edinburgh, local Anti-Poll Tax groups started a
campaign, called Operation Suburban Storm,
to visit local councillors' homes and carry out
mock poindings.

Occupations were another common tactic
of the campaign against the bailiffs and the
councils. On September 20th 1989, Edinburgh
activists took over the council chamber when
the Labour council decided to go ahead with
warrant sales. On November 17th, they occupied the offices of Sheriff Officer H.M. Love.
Similar actions took place in Glasgow. On October 12th over 50 Glasgow Anti-Poll Tax protesters occupied the offices of sheriff officers
Gray and Scott. This occupation (which was
organised by the Strathclyde Anti-Poll Tax
Federation) demanded that a threatened warrant sale against a woman, Mrs. Patton was
dropped. Within three hours the sheriffs
agreed to drop the case and hand it back to the
council. The level of activity grew more intense:

In Strathclyde there have been at least
four occupations of sheriff officers' offices.
On April 18th the offices of George Walker
(sheriff officers) were occupied by 40
people For over 28 hours. In the following
week, three other sheriffs' offices were
occupied, including one by Pollock Against
The Poll Tax on 23rd April. On 11th May,
40 people occupied an Easterhouse DSS
office for 10 hours to protest at Poll Tax
deductions from claimants' benefits.
Counter Information, No.27, June 1990.

While these were all serious political actions, many of them had a funny side. John Cooper from Glasgow describes an occupation of the Poll Tax Office on Queen Street:

We had about 30 people and it was quite well-organised. So we went through the office, and I happened to notice that there were still people arriving to pay their Poll Tax. The staff had all kinda moved back out of the way, so I just sat down at the desk and said through the glass, 'Can I help you?' I says 'It's OK you don't need to pay any more, its abolished!' and the guy says, 'Are you sure?' I says, 'I'm positive, you know what I'd do with this money, go and spend it, have a good time.' He says, 'You're having me on.' I could see the guy was still uncertain. So there was a bunch of pads for phone messages, I ripped one of them off, and said' 'If there's any bother just send that in to us.'

Demonstrators occupy the

offices of Edinburgh bailiffs

Gray and Scott.

John Cooper, Glasgow, 8/5/91.

Rob Houn

By April 1991 (after the Poll Tax had been introduced for a year), few bailiff companies had recovered enough to survive on. Bristol City Council for example had only received £54,000 in response to their threatening letters (from a total of over 120,000 non-payers). As long as non-payment held up, the odds were dramatically stacked against the bailiffs. There were simply not enough of them to deal with the problem. At their 1990 annual conference, Simon Smith, the Secretary of the Association of Certified Bailiffs, admitted that with only 1000 registered bailiffs and over 10 million expected non-payers they didn't have a chance of enforcing even a small fraction.

The biggest problem for the bailiffs was that they were paid on a commission basis. If they didn't recover the Poll Tax debt for the council, they didn't get paid for the work they did. This proved troublesome, not least because they had lost the safe source of income which they used to receive from the rates. Many bailiff firms faced serious cash flow problems as they needed to employ more people but received less money. A report in the *Hackney Gazette* high-lighted their problem:

> Rayner Ferrar and Co., whose contract ended this week, added that they faced bankruptcy if they had continued working for the Town Hall. David Rayner, a director of the bailiff company, said: 'We had 15,000 liability orders given to us to chase up. Four out of five of all those liability orders were not collectable because the Poll Tax register is in such a terrible mess. People named in the register weren't at the address given, or they were paying by direct debit and it wasn't on the computer, or they were liable for rebates they hadn't received. We desperately need accurate financial information. It is not financially viable for us to act for Hackney Council any longer, we'll go bust if we continue.' Town Hall bosses have refused to agree to the new terms the bailiffs demanded – a set payment for every case they chased up

whether of not the rebel paid up, plus the agreed commission. Previously they worked on a commission only basis.
Hackney Gazette, 19/4/91.

In the South-West two bailiff firms went out of business. This was not uncommon elsewhere. By July 1981, when the tax had been in place for more than two years, Scottish bailiffs had carried out 41,102 poinding visits (*Labour Research*, October 1991) but they hadn't managed to sell the goods of a single one, and, in England and Wales, the number of successful bailiff actions could be counted on the fingers of one hand.

Defying The Threat Of Income Deduction

In many cases the appeal of attachment of earnings orders to the government parallels the appeal of the charge. Both are deceptively simple and in an ideal world, where good citizens follow their statutory duties on time, and with attention to detail, then the problems so obvious to practical collectors evaporate. Unfortunately, it is the collectors' view which is closer to the real world, not the government's
Local Government Chronicle, Poll Tax supplement, 16/11/90.

The alternative to bailiff action was wage arrestment, income support arrestment and, in Scotland, the freezing of bank accounts. Local councils had the power to instruct employers and the Department of Social Security to deduct money directly from people's incomes. A number of high profile actions were taken against income support deductions such as the occupation and roof-top protest carried out by Tottenham Anti-Poll Tax Union on 17th July 1991, but the focus of activity was on practical advice and attempts to get the trade unions to resist.

Anti-Poll Tax Unions advised their members to take their money out of the four big banks and use smaller banks or building societies. In some cases, even bank staff warned people that their accounts would be frozen, so they moved their money elsewhere. In the end, the banks made it clear to local councils that freezing bank accounts was not an effective enforcement procedure and they would not co-operate indefinitely:

> The Committee of Scottish Clearing Bankers has written to the regional councils urging them not to proceed with mass account arrestments. The banks are particularly worried about mass speculative arrestments where sheriff officers send lists of names to bank head offices in the hope that some of the people named will have bank accounts. The banks have to circulate the lists to branches who have to check their records. The 'success rate' according to the Committee is only around 5-6%.
> *LGIU, Poll Tax Focus, No.11, December 1989.*

As a result bank account freezing was not included in the enforcement options when the Poll Tax was introduced to England and Wales.

Wage arrestment on the other hand, appeared to offer some chance of success, but it turned out to be just as problematic. In the first instance, it didn't act as a deterrent for people on low incomes because there was a maximum amount that councils could deduct each week. This operated on a sliding scale but could be no more than £1.75 per week for those on income support, and £8 per week for someone earning £100. So, even if someone did get their wages arrested, they would end up paying less per week than if they paid the Poll Tax direct. This meant that there was an incentive to wait.

The threat of trade union action was also a potential problem for councils. Attempts to resist wage arrestment through union action were focused around setting up work-place

163

Anti-Poll Tax Unions. These bypassed official trade union structures, because even those few unions such as NALGO who had a theoretical policy of support for non-payment, refused to put it into practice. A number of work-places set up groups, but these ran up against heavy resistance. George Thorne, of the Stockport branch of 'Postal Workers Against The Poll Tax' highlighted some of the difficulties in an article for *Socialist Voice*:

> We borrowed some union notepaper and put up a notice asking anyone who was interested to attend a meeting. The meeting was well-attended and we formed our group calling ourselves The UCW Anti-Poll Tax Group. Almost immediately we came into collision with the UCW. The Union said that we should not have used union headed notepaper. In the August edition of our union newspaper *The Post*, there was a small unsigned article advising members not to support PWAPT.

This was a typical union reaction and these organisational problems ensured that only a few work-place groups thrived. There was some strike action by council workers, but it tended, like the strike of Greenwich housing workers, to be more related to improving the working conditions of Poll Tax office staff than challenging the Poll Tax itself. As a result, there were very few examples of unions and employers who refused to deduct from wages.

However, the councils still had one insurmountable headache. They had to find out where people worked. This was a real nightmare because other than asking the people concerned, they had no real way of getting the information they needed. When a liability order was granted by the court, non-payers were sent a form which requested details of employment. Failure to fill it out carried a fine of £100 and £400 if the non-payer provided false information. But this didn't act as a deterrent either, because, if people couldn't pay the Poll Tax itself (and the court costs which were added), then it made little difference if the council added another £100. A survey carried out by the Audit Commission in late 1989 showed that, nationally, only 15% of people who received the form actually sent it back. Like electoral registration, it was widely ignored even though this was a criminal offence. As a result it was difficult for the councils to arrest the wages of anyone other than those employed by large institutions (their own employees, colleges of further education, and some large corporations), but these only represented a small fraction of non-payers.

By July 1991, Scottish local authorities had only managed 14,102 wage arrestments and 14,710 bank arrestments (*Labour Research*, October 1990) which, from a population of over a million Scottish non-payers, was laughable. They achieved more income support deductions (72,819 by June 1991) but, because of the small amounts involved, it cost councils more to administer them than they got back. Councils in England and Wales could do no better. Now, their only hope of recovering the money was to threaten imprisonment.

Too Many People To Jail

The threat of imprisonment was the final deterrent aimed at intimidating people into paying. The first person threatened was a 74-year old pensioner, Mr. Cyril Mundin. He was arrested on Thursday 11th October 1990, by bailiffs from the firm of Madigans. After spending one and a half hours at the local police station, he was escorted to the magistrates' court, where he was given fourteen days to pay his outstanding tax. He was threatened with a fourteen-day prison sentence if he refused to comply. Bailiffs had unsuccessfully attempted to enter his house on three occasions. Activists,

165

angered by the action of Northampton Borough Council, occupied the offices of the City Treasurer, refusing to let him go for over an hour. In the end, Mr. Mundin didn't go to jail, his Poll Tax was paid by *The News of the World*. This action was not a spontaneous gesture of sympathy, it was an attempt to deflect the bad publicity which the jailing of a pensioner would have received.

It was not long before the first non-payer was jailed. On Friday 7th December, Brian Wright was jailed for 21 days by Grantham Council. Brian received over 800 cards and letters from well-wishers, 700 demonstrators turned up outside the prison a week later and the local council was inundated by hate mail from Anti-Poll Tax activists. Douglas Hogg, the local MP and government minister was visited by twenty people including members of the Wright family. Through pressure, they forced the MP to ensure that Brian was allowed to be visited every day, and he was released after only fourteen days. Political pressure of this sort, surprisingly seemed to have an impact on the conditions of imprisoned non-payers and some had their sentences reduced.

The second non-payer to be jailed was Patrick Westmore on the Isle of Wight. Patrick was a Militant supporter and Chair of the local Anti-Poll Tax Union. While he demonstrated that he only had £36.70 a week to live on, he was still imprisoned for fourteen days – clearly singled out because of his political role. By September 1991, 70 people had been sent to prison for non-payment, mostly for a couple of weeks but in some cases up to three months. The Labour MP, Terry Fields, was imprisoned for two months. Regular pickets were mounted outside the prisons. In many areas, the local prisoners' support groups, which had formed after the Trafalgar Square demonstration, carried out similar work for non-payment prisoners. They arranged visits, sent cards and books, and ensured that letters and statements from the prisoners were published.

For those who were not in a position to make a principled stand, the committal hearings were important because magistrates were obliged to take into account the financial circumstances of the defendants. So, far from acting as a deterrent, some people saw them as the only chance they would get to explain their financial circumstances to the authorities. Defendants had the right to a full means hearing and had the opportunity to present their family accounts. This meant that it was in the interest of everyone (even those who decided that they would eventually pay) to wait until the committal hearing, because they were likely to get a more favourable instalment deal from the court than the council.

In addition to this, at the commital stage, magistrates had the right to waive debts. On 26th February 1991, Sharon West a mother of three children was brought before the Taunton Deane Magistrates' Court for non-payment. If she had been imprisoned, her children would have been put into care. The magistrates let her walk free. Other magistrates were not so sympathetic, apparently unable to comprehend the poverty people faced:

The Finneys offered to pay £5 a week. The magistrate said that it wasn't enough. He wanted to know why Mr. Finney, who is a labourer for a pottery firm, spent £10 per week travelling to work. 'Didn't he have a company car?'
Newcastle Under Lyme Magistrates' Court, June 1991.

Mark Simmons

Even when they were summoned to court for committal to prison, very few people turned up.

167

While the number of people facing prison appeared frighteningly high, the situation had actually been far worse under the rates. Unknown to most people, an average of over 300 people a year had been imprisoned for inability to pay the rates over the previous ten years (Stoke on Trent CAB, survey, 1987). Now for the first time the councils had been forced to expose what they were doing.

Because imprisonment was the last stage of the enforcement process, councils needed it to be an effective deterrent. So, officials of Labour councils stood up in court and argued for people to be imprisoned, even where the non-payer offered to have their wages arrested or tried to pay in monthly instalments. But still people were not deterred. In September 1991, Bristol City Council started taking 40 people a week through the courts for committal hearings. A local councillor, Robin Moss (one of the rebels expelled from the Labour Group for his stand against the Poll Tax), managed to get hold of the list of those due to appear. He noticed the name of someone he knew on the list, and immediately rang her up. 'Did you realise you are due to appear in court tomorrow for a committal hearing?'. 'Oh yes' she replied, 'but I have to take some kids to see the dinosaurs.' This captures the mood of indifference to the actions of the authorities. Of that first 40 people, five came to an agreement with the council before the court case, five cases were heard (four were given suspended sentences and one was imprisoned), but the other 30 didn't bother to turn up. They could technically be arrested by bailiffs (and one or two were) but it was impossible to track them all down.

The Bristol cases were instructive for another reason. The first man to be sent down, Tony Whitfield, was held for three days in a police cell in Frome because there was no room in any of the Bristol police stations or in Bristol's Horfield Jail. The second man imprisoned, David Britain, was sent to a police station in Hampshire, because, there was no space available anywhere in Avon. The third, Paul Chamberlain, was taken to a police station in

Bridgwater and then transferred to Plymouth. So, if the authorities were having trouble dealing with the first three cases, how were they going to deal with the hundreds who had already been given suspended sentences, let alone the 150,000 non-payers waiting to be summoned? It is worth adding that it cost the government around £600 per week to put people in jail, so for each two-month sentence they were paying over £5,000 in lieu of perhaps £500 unpaid Poll Tax.

Most councils quickly realised that it would be impossible to imprison more than a handful of people and slackened off the pace of committal hearings, but the public also realised this, and knew that there was now no effective sanction against non-payment. The State was reduced to the futile mass production of threatening letters which were increasingly ignored by an angry and confident population.

A tired but defiant Tony Whitfield emerges from prison after being refused medication for four days.

Mark Simmons

169

Sinking The Flagship

So I say: let us have some recriminations.
This was not some natural unforeseen
disaster. Everything that happened to this
miserable, misbegotten, mean spirited
piece of legislation was predicted right from
the start. Even large sections of the Conservative Party especially in local government, warned privately of what would
happen. But most shamefully kept quiet in
public because Mummy wanted it, and
Mummy knew best. Can one even begin to
imagine the outcry there would have been
in the Tory newspapers if a Labour government had made such a catastrophic mess?

So let Messrs. Baker, Ridley, Portillo,
Gummer, Howard, Patten and the rest be
forced to parade through the streets
wearing placards, dunces' caps and red
noses. Let them be beaten about the head
with pigs' bladders. Let the Thatcher
Foundation be presented with a bill for
£3,390m. Let all members of the Adam
Smith Institute be debarred from holding
public office in their life-times. And let every
Right-wing scribbler and leader writer who
defended the tax attend a great televised
banquet at which they are required to eat
their words without the benefit of alcohol.
Robert Harris, Sunday Times, 24/2/91.

The events I have narrated describe the
downfall of the Poll Tax. Crippled by the im-
possibility of enforcement, the government
was forced to back down. This section chroni-
cles the way in which that happened.

From the beginning of 1990, the government went through a series of tactical retreats.
Month after month, minor modifications were
made to reduce the burden of taxation on this
group or that. In February 1990, following the
Town Hall riots and a series of opinion polls

which showed overwhelming public opposition to the Poll Tax, Thatcher ordered her Environment Secretary, Chris Patten, to investigate further changes:

> Ministers privately admit that the chaotic run up to April's introduction of the Community Charge is proving so politically damaging that changes will have to be made.
> *The Observer, 18/2/90.*

But this was not to be a 'root and branch' review. Its purpose was still to sort out the 'anomalies', and the Tories continued to defend the principle of the Poll Tax.

On March 25th the *Sunday Correspondent* produced an opinion poll which showed that Michael Heseltine (a consistent opponent of the Poll Tax) would reduce Labour's lead in the polls if he were to become leader of the Conservative Party:

> Even more remarkable is the demonstration of Mr. Heseltine's electoral potency. Labour's standing in the poll is 55% compared with 28% for the Tories, but when voters were asked how they would vote if Heseltine were Conservative leader the lead narrowed dramatically to 48% for Labour, 41% for the Conservatives.
> *Sunday Correspondent, 25/3/90.*

He began to talk openly of his reservations about the Poll Tax but still refused to challenge the Prime Minister, pledging support for her and the party:

> I have made it clear many times that I expect Mrs. Thatcher to lead the party into the next election and that the Conservatives will win.
> *Sunday Correspondent, 25/3/91.*

But, his carefully worded statements served only to fuel press speculation about a possible leadership challenge.

In April 1990, following the Trafalgar

Square demonstration, the Tories lost the key Mid-Staffordshire by-election with a swing to Labour of 21.3% – the biggest swing from Conservative to Labour since the Putney by-election of 1934.

The May local council elections produced a mixed result. The Labour Party had a substantial overall victory (albeit not as big as predicted), gaining over 300 council seats, but it was tarnished by an effective Tory propaganda campaign which focused solely on the results of their two 'flagship' local authorities, Westminster and Wandsworth. These two authorities had managed to get their Poll Tax level down to £176 and £149 per head. Both authorities increased their share of the vote and the Tories were able to argue that the problem with the Poll Tax was that Labour authorities were spending too much and setting their Poll Tax too high. They argued that people were not rejecting the principle of the Poll Tax, but the level. The argument was flawed because the Labour Party increased its share of the vote in Haringey which had the highest Poll Tax level in Britain. Also both Westminster and Wandsworth received far greater central government subsidy than virtually any other councils. Nevertheless, the Tories scored a propaganda victory which enabled them to struggle on with the Poll Tax, maintaining the belief that if they ironed out the anomalies, and imposed limits on Labour's ability to spend through capping, then they would see out the political difficulties.

Over the next months, as non-payment quietly mounted and the enforcement process began, trouble for the Tories opened on a different front. The deputy Prime Minister, Geoffrey Howe, made a mortally wounding speech in the House of Commons attacking Thatcher for her position on Europe and exposing her autocratic style of government. This speech opened up the floodgates. It was swiftly followed by an attack from Nigel Lawson, her ex-Chancellor, who also attacked the Poll Tax. The door was finally opened for Michael Heseltine to challenge for the leadership. The main election

Mark Simmons

issue was the Poll Tax. Thatcher won the first ballot, but failed to gain an overall majority. The 'Iron Lady' was wounded, and it soon became clear that many Tory MPs would no longer support her . On November 20th 1990, Thatcher reluctantly withdrew from the leadership contest and resigned as Prime Minister. John Major was elected as the new party leader, and, in a bid for party unity, brought Michael Heseltine into the cabinet, giving him responsibility for reforming the Poll Tax.

Major authorised Heseltine to carry out a fundamental review of the tax. But he also made it clear that he didn't intend to abolish it. When he was asked on TV AM's Frost on Sunday whether he would veto a proposal from Michael Heseltine to abolish the tax, he said, 'I am sure he won't suggest that, the situation won't arise.'

On March 7th 1991, the Liberal Democrats won the Tories fourth safest seat at the Ribble Valley by-election, overturning a majority of 19,528 to win by over 4,000 votes. All the opinion polls carried out in the weeks preceding the election showed that the overriding issue of concern was the Poll Tax. This was a deeply

Above:

People refused to be bought

off by sweeteners which

they could see were short

term.

173

worrying sign for Tory Party election strategists. In the year since its introduction the government had been forced to extend rebates to more and more people, and had widened the scope of relief payments. Neither of these changes had dampened down public anger. Changes now had to be made which were more than cosmetic:

> Mr. Major has admitted that there must be something wrong with a tax which starts with the principle that everyone should pay, and ends with a system under which 18m out of 36m have to be offered rebates to damp the political furore.
> *Financial Times, 21/2/91.*

Thatcher resigns. A day of rejoicing for the many people who had suffered under Thatcherism.

These were made possible by the new budget of the Chancellor Norman Lamont. On March 19th he announced that every Poll Tax bill in the country would be reduced by £140. This reduction was to be paid for by a 2.5% increase in VAT - an initiative designed to take the sting out of the resistance to the Poll Tax. But because

Mark Simmons

it involved recalculating 35 million bills it created even deeper administrative chaos for the
councils. It also created the perverse situation
in which residents of Wandsworth didn't have
to pay any tax. This was widely resented. Over
the following week the Tory Party furiously
debated the future of the Poll Tax. The Right-
wing clung faithfully to the principle that
'everyone should pay something.' As a result, a
hybrid tax was touted around the corridors of
Westminster, a tax which would be partly a
head tax and partly a property tax. This too was
attacked from within the Tory ranks - described by Nigel Lawson as the 'son of Poll
Tax'.

On Thursday March 21st, Michael
Heseltine announced the abolition of the Poll
Tax. He said it would be replaced in 1993, by a
new taxation system based on ability to pay.
This new 'Council Tax' was to be a banded tax
based on property value.

The Anti-Poll Tax movement celebrated,
but remained firm in its commitment to non-
payment as it was still two years before the new
tax would be introduced. They knew that if
people couldn't pay the first years Poll Tax
there was no possibility of them paying a second or third. It was also difficult to predict how
progressive the new Council Tax would actually turn out to be.

The political parties all declared that the
victory was theirs. The Liberal Democrats
proclaimed that the Ribble Valley by-election
was the reason why the Poll Tax was abolished.

This victory for the Liberal Democrats has
put paid to the Poll Tax. If there was any
doubt that it was the issue that was going
to settle this by-election then there's no
doubt now. When the Poll Tax is finally laid
to rest in the grave, its epitaph will read:
'Here lies the Poll Tax killed in Ribble
Valley'.
Mike Carr, Elected MP for Ribble Valley, The Guardian, 8/3/91.

They failed to admit that the reason for their
victory was the vibrant campaign mounted by

the non-payment movement. But the Prime Minister John Major made it quite clear why the tax had been abolished. In his address to concerned Right-wingers, a week before the announcement of abolition, he said that the Poll Tax was unenforceable. He cited figures of 17.5 million people who had either not paid or were in serious arrears – about half of those liable to pay. As *The Observer* reported:

> If the Poll Tax is dead it was killed by non-payment, a tactic which each of the three main parties insisted was pointless and wrong. Extra-parliamentary action, that nightmare of Westminster politicians, proved itself and in the process exposed the hollowness of our claims to democracy... This weekend each and every one of those non-payers should feel proud of themselves... The SNP can claim more credit from the affair than most, but their non-payment campaign was never the true engine of the revolt. The much trumpeted 'list of 100,000' non-payers was never convincing and some of the party's own councillors buckled when faced with hard choices... Labour councillors... shed crocodile tears which would have shamed a Nile crocodile while inviting non-payers to take a close look at the law's teeth... Few of Scotland's politicians have anything to be proud of at the end of this episode. When most needed they were found wanting and it was left to a rag-tag army of ordinary people to destroy a bad law.
> *The Observer, 24/3/91.*

What a powerful army it proved to be! The publication of the first 1991 report on the Poll Tax by the Audit Commission must have made sobering reading. By the end of January, non-payment averaged 18% in shire district councils, 27% in metropolitan districts, 23% in outer London boroughs and 34% in inner London boroughs. Most councils were borrowing heavily to bridge the gap. In Scotland, non-payment had almost doubled from 18% in the first year to nearly 35%. In England and Wales, even when people had been through the courts, only 28% of people paid up when they received liability orders. And it was not only the non-payers who were causing trouble. The Poll Tax Legal Group, who attended an Audit Commission conference on enforcing the Poll Tax, reported a number of interesting insights:

The conference revealed the existence of a vast unorganised protest movement who are sabotaging the community charge quite independently of the existing non-payment campaigns. These include people who are paying only their old rates' bills, people who are deducting the transitional relief portion of their demands and people

Mark Simmons

paying direct debit who run 'disorderly
accounts' whereby no or insufficient money
is to be found in them when payment is
due.
Poll Tax Legal Group, Law Review No.4, March 1991.

In 1991, following the announcement of
abolition, non-payment levels in many of the
big cities of Britain rose even higher. In many
London boroughs, Strathclyde, Bristol and
other large cities it rose above 50%. People were
not going to pay a tax which had been abolished because of its unfairness. Thatcher and
the Poll Tax had been brought down by a
people's campaign which was persistently dismissed by the political establishment until it
exploded with a force that was unstoppable.

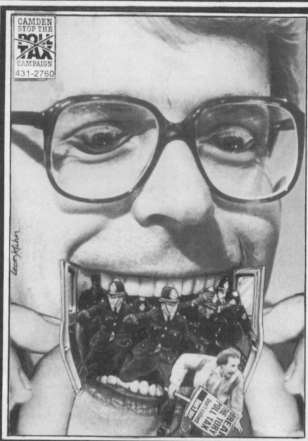

6

AFTER THE POLL TAX: WHAT IS LEFT?

Mark Simmons

Betrayal And Power

The defeat of the Poll Tax was one of the greatest demonstrations of ' people power' in modern political history. In many respects it was comparable with recent events in Eastern Europe. But it is not yet certain that it has resulted in lasting changes. Having beaten back one of the most important symbols of Thatcherism, we certainly have more confidence and we have learnt important lessons about how to organise political struggle. Nevertheless, capitalism has been able to carry on pretty much as usual. The government continues to attack the welfare state; the national taxation system remains heavily weighted in favour of the rich; and the number of people imprisoned, because they cannot pay debts, is still staggeringly high. The Poll Tax was a symbol around which people were able to focus their anger and action, but the principles which underlay the Poll Tax still remain to be fought. Jim Kelman, a Glasgow based writer reminds us:

> Nothing was ever given freely by the ruling class, not in this country or any other country. When left with no alternative they concede, but when given the chance, what they concede, they retrieve – they fight tooth and nail to claw back.
>
> *Jim Kelman, 4th Scottish Anti-Poll Tax Forum, 11/5/91.*

So, we have to make sure that we are able build on the success of this campaign, to address the more fundamental issues of inequality and injustice - issues which relate to a capitalist system based on individualism and greed.

The first thing to be clear about is, that we have only ourselves to rely on. We were not only nakedly attacked by the Tories, but were betrayed by the official labour movement which purported to represent us. Many who were prepared to consider resistance, were instructed by the Labour Party to capitulate:

182

This area is Labour, there's no getting away
from it. Their fathers voted Labour, their
grandfathers voted Labour, it's always been
Labour. It probably always will be Labour.
Before the tax came in there was talk that
they would oppose it. But as soon as the
Party said, 'you must pay,' they paid.

Chris Moyers, Mayfield APTU, 6/5/91.

That we succeeded in bringing about an act of
collective civil disobedience, which involved
over 17 million people, when all the main political parties and most national trade unions
were attempting to undermine it, not only
demonstrates our collective strength, it also
highlights the chronic weakness of the official
labour movement.

From the very start, they argued that we
would never build a community campaign
because there was no longer a community.
They said that people were only interested in
themselves and didn't go to meetings; that
people were demoralised by the political de-
feats of the last decade and would not be prepared to take risks over the Poll Tax and, that
people in Britain might demonstrate, but
would never be convinced not to pay because
they were law-abiding citizens with no tradition of breaking the law:

The message coming in from just about
every party is clearer than it's ever been.
Not just from the mainstream but also from
the fringe left parties. What they're saying
is, genuine social change is not possible, all
we have left is compromise and negotiation. Whatever the fight was in the past, it's
rear guard nowadays, cling onto what you
have in the face of irresistible forces. Only
the loonies think other wise, dewy-eyed
idealists and sentimental fools, people who
live in a dream world.

Jim Kelman, 4th Scottish Anti-Poll Tax Forum, 11/5/91.

Yet millions of people broke the law for the first
time. Local communities turned out against the
bailiffs; hundreds of thousands went to meet-

ings; and many more contributed in other ways. Individuals and communities took the risks that the labour movement was not prepared to take.

Throughout the '80s many Labour councillors adopted a pragmatic position, admitting that they were managing the Tories' cuts in services, but arguing that they needed to be there to protect the most vulnerable from the impact of those cuts. The Poll Tax put this argument to the test, because it was those who couldn't pay who needed the services the most. Yet, despite the fact that some magistrates and even Tory councillors resigned (in Oxfordshire 18 Tory councillors stepped down in protest against the tax), only a handful of Labour councillors followed suit.

Few people in the Anti-Poll Tax movement expected local councils to take a lead. However, given that by the autumn of 1990, non-payment was running at over 20% in virtually every urban area (and was much higher in many big cities) some elements in the Labour Party mainstream might have been expected to break ranks and back the non-payment campaign. But not a single council did. All sent bailiffs and sheriff officers to the homes of those who couldn't pay – the same 'vulnerable' people, Labour said, they were there to protect.

It is likely that most Labour voters were non-payers since 17 million British people refused to pay the Poll Tax and less than 11 million voted Labour in the 1987 General Election. Given this it seems politically perverse that the Labour Party chose to attack its potential electorate. It was a strategy presumably founded on the arrogant belief that the inner-city electorate would vote Labour, whatever policies were presented to them.

They said that they were forced by law to implement the tax (and would face surcharge and disqualification from office if they refused to comply) but none of them actually tested or even checked this out. Some argued that it would be unwise for them to stick their heads above the parapet after the failed resistance to rate capping, but in reality, it was only Liver-

pool and Lambeth that resisted that government attack, and they didn't have a mass
movement of 17 million people behind them. If
Labour had either resigned or refused to implement the tax, the Tories would have been
forced to up the stakes, either by running Labour areas themselves or bringing in un-
elected commissioners. This would have provoked even greater anger and would almost
certainly have led to wider action (particularly
in the work-place). By mid-1990, when it was
obvious to all urban councils that non-payment
was massive, they would clearly have been in a
position to take action with the support of the
population. So they did have a choice! Why is it
then that they refused to stand with the people?

Many officials of the Labour Party were
simply afraid of jeopardising their careers.
Some feared losing control to a mass move-

ment which acted both spontaneously and un-
predictably – a movement which couldn't be
manipulated because of its sheer size.

Other Labour Party activists genuinely believed that real power lay with central government. They justified the way in which they
cynically laid aside their principles, by arguing

that they would put everything right as soon as they got elected. What this meant in practice was that people who couldn't afford to pay the Poll Tax would have to be sacrificed until after the next general election. What they failed to grasp was the fundamental difference between being elected and having power.

While it is true to say that class distinctions are less easy to define than they used to be, it remains indisputable that only a small fraction of the population own the vast majority of Britain's wealth. These privileged people will do anything to hold onto it, and they have the support of powerful interest groups to fight on their behalf (big business, the media, the police and the military). When Labour threatened to introduce a minimum wage, the Director General of the CBI didn't rush off to the Conservatives and ask them to mount a protest campaign. He simply announced that Industry would disinvest in the British economy making it impossible for Labour to run it (Question Time, Radio 4, 13/10/91). Large corporations consistently fail to pay their taxes. It is well-known that senior civil servants have undermined Labour legislation. Likewise, it is common knowledge that the secret services have acted to topple Labour governments. All this is direct action. None of it has anything to do with parliamentary democracy. But the Labour party are powerless to do anything about it, and in most cases turn a blind eye. Their suggestion during the campaign, that they couldn't support a movement which was operating outside of the law was laughable. The Tories have always done so. They use parliament to introduce legislation supporting their interests, but they know that the power to enforce it lies elsewhere. Labour's failure to recognise this has reduced them to an organ of protest and negotiation - appealing to the 'decency' of powerful people who are concerned about little other than making money.

To clarify: to fight the forces of oppression it is necessary to have a counter force with which to resist them. Promises, policies, negotiation and even legislation don't constitute a

Mark Simmons

force. The only force we have is people and their power to take collective action. This was what non-payment was about. Because the community was physically withholding something which the state needed, it was exercising power. Because it was based in local neighbourhoods, and authority was not vested in the representative structures, that power was not diluted, and it couldn't be corrupted. The vicious response of the state, indicated just how seriously it took the threat:

> The very fact that the state employs the forces of law and order so consistently, to check direct action by the public, gives the lie to the notion that radical change is not possible. If it was not possible, the authorities would scarcely respond with such consistent ruthlessness. Radical change is always possible.
> *Jim Kelman, 4th Scottish Anti-Poll Tax Forum, 11/5/91.*

Confidence And
Political Motivation

Recognising the importance of resistance, and realising that the battle had to be fought outside of the labour movement were important steps for activists. But the first priority was to convince ordinary people that it was worth fighting. Often they were cynical about political action because they had been consistently told by the labour movement that they couldn't win. They were also given the impression that the consequences of non-co-operation would be devastating. Many genuinely feared the sheriff officers:

> People who live in this community, they remember the days, as I can remember as a child, where if you didn'y pay your rent everything was put out on the street, on the cart, and that was you - in the days of the landlords. I mean I was brought up in a single end, you had no facilities, you lived in one room, you shared your facilities with everyone else who lived in what had been a house and had been sub-let into various small apartments. They remember that, and were never so glad to get a council house.
>
> *Linda Wright, Prestonfield Community Resistance, 10/5/91.*

Some feared that the homes which they had spent their lives working for, could be taken from them. The political parties colluded in this disinformation. The Anti-Poll Tax movement had to counter it, and convince people that if they stood together they could win.

Giving people this confidence was essential, because it was only once they believed that it was possible to create change that they could take action. Unless people have a vision of what might be, and how they might achieve it, it is too painful for them to acknowledge the daily

188

oppression they face. Anything other than re-sistance will be a half-way house which simply serves to remind people of their circumstances, while telling them that they cannot be changed. This is why no-one was interested in the Labour Party 'Stop It' campaign. People aren't motivated by 'sensibleness' or spurred into action by 'realism'. They need to know that their imaginative visions might actually become reality.

The issue of nuclear war is a persistent illustration of this. People are universally frightened by the possibility of global annihilation but, because the scale of the problem is so big, they see no way of challenging it. It takes on an air of inevitability which is so terrifying that people would rather pretend that the problem didn't exist. They turn over the pages of newspapers or switch television programmes, rather than face reality. When confronted, they may even argue in favour of nuclear weapons because by doing so they no longer have to deal with feelings of impotence.

Papers like *The Sun* aren't only popular because they are a quick read, people like them because they offer the possibility that life can change. In the tabloid world anything is possible. For those who work in boring jobs, this can be a breath of fresh air. The lotteries and competitions offer a way out of the nightmare of poverty. The images of wealth allow people to fantasise about how life might be. The 'quality' newspapers don't allow imagination. Everything is 'fact'. Our depressing reality is described in detail, but no possibilities for change are offered. Traditional Left-wing politics tends to be the same, failing to understand just how close imagination, confidence and vision are to the process of effecting political change. The fact that people were not encouraged to build visions was the first hurdle that Anti-Poll Tax campaigners had to deal with, yet as soon as a realistic programme for radical change was outlined, people wanted to know more.

Once people were motivated to act, the most important thing was to keep them involved. Prior to the Anti-Poll Tax campaign, many people's only experience of politics was a traditional Labour Party or trade union meeting - the sort of meeting where the top table takes up 90% of the discussion; where the only items discussed are those decided by the executive committee; where half the meeting time is spent discussing procedural motions or the order of words in a resolution; where political factions throw rhetoric across the room in angry and unproductive exchanges. Essentially, boring meetings which stretch long into the night. Hundreds of thousands of people have been to these meetings just once and never returned. To engage people in a mass campaign, the Anti-Poll Tax Unions had to challenge this culture of organisation. They had to make people feel wanted and included and give everyone a sense that they had a role. In order to sustain a long and protracted struggle, it was necessary for as many people as possible to feel responsible for some aspect of the movement, however small. In the fight against the bailiffs and sheriff officers, the kids hanging around the streets passed on the word as soon as they saw a suspicious-looking character. Parents and pensioners who were not out at work, organised telephone trees and were ready to be outside each others' houses at short notice. They didn't have to go to meetings in order to organise. Information could get passed on in other ways:

> Leeds City Council has a policy of blacking out all the posters of rock concerts and things like that. Somebody from the Hyde Park group thought they made excellent blackboards and started chalking out explanations on how you delay registration in different coloured chalks with little pictures. It really worked. I could see people coming back from the pub standing there for about five or ten minutes reading all these different messages.
> *Ian Greaves, Leeds Federation APTUs, 11/5/91.*

This immediate form of organisation also meant that people weren't patronised by those who had political experience. In the local groups, people didn't need permission to act, they just had to get on the phone to their neighbours and get something going. People stay involved in political campaigns if they can contribute in the way that *they* feel is most effective. Very often this is not by sitting in boring meetings.

People have different experiences and skills, so they need to operate in different ways to be effective. This means that political movements have to accommodate a great deal of diversity. Because of this, most of the successful Anti-Poll Tax Unions operated on a principle of parallel development. Rather than trying to assert majority control or spend hours reaching consensus, people were allowed to get on with what they thought was most important. Everything could be done in the name of the Anti-Poll Tax Union, which existed to co-ordinate activity against the Poll Tax, not to specify its exact nature.

Underlying this approach is a belief that it is not necessary to have a single uniform direc-

It was ordinary people – people who weren't interested in long boring meetings – who formed the back-bone of the campaign. So new methods of organising had to be found to keep them involved.

Mark Simmons

191

tion or strategy to be politically effective. Indeed, sometimes strategies which appear to be contradictory can actually reinforce each other. The Anti-Poll Tax movement encompassed an enormous range of approaches:

- People who were not prepared to break the law.
- People who threw petrol bombs at Poll Tax Offices.
- Mass door to door leafletting
- The bugging of computers.
- Harassment of bailiffs and council snoopers.
- Occupations of courts and council chambers.
- Technical legal challenges in the courts.

The activities of those who were not prepared to break the law were not undermined by the actions of the few who chose to throw fire bombs. Likewise, those who chose to leave Trafalgar Square peacefully, were not tarnished by those who chose to fight back against the police attack. The occupations of the courts didn't prevent those who wanted to argue legal technicalities, and those who chose not to attend meetings but to take action on their own, didn't undermine the collective decisions of those who met in the APTUs. The movement was not damaged by this diversity, it was strengthened by it. It created a feeling that everyone, from every walk of life, was involved in this campaign in some way, and that meant it was strong.

Political Leadership

In spite of the lack of central leadership, there was a remarkable consensus across Britain about the sorts of direct action to take. In other words, we didn't need a central leadership to tell us what to do – given the existence of oppression and

injustice, people's response has a logical momentum of its own, and people behave consistently in struggle.
Glen Burrows, Bridgwater APTU, June 1991.

The Anti-Poll Tax campaign had no unified political leadership and yet it was extraordinarily successful. In most political movements instructions and information travel up and down the organisational hierarchy; key decisions and debates are carried out by regional and national executives. What was unique about the Anti-Poll Tax campaign was the degree of direct interaction and decision-making which occurred at a local level.

There was, for example, no need for a policy directive to establish the various strategies of non-co-operation. People understood the need for it – many had no choice. This is illustrated by the fact that it was sometimes in the places where the Anti-Poll Tax Unions were weakest that resistance was strongest. For example, St. Pauls was almost the only area in Bristol which couldn't sustain an Anti-Poll Tax group. Local people didn't feel the need to set up new groups because, as in many inner city areas, they already had strong networks of solidarity, and there was already a high level of general hostility to officials of any sort. So the bailiffs didn't dare walk down most streets, let alone attempt distraint. By the end of 1990, three times as many people had turned up to court to contest their cases from St. Pauls than any other area. The neighbouring Anti-Poll Tax Unions provided information and helped to create a visible atmosphere of defiance, but the consensus not to co-operate resulted from local communication through informal networks.

In this situation the most effective leadership will not tell people what to do – they usually know what needs to be done – but will give people the confidence to do it. This means providing information and ideas so that people can make choices, and helping them to set up groups so that they can share experiences and provide each other with solidarity. It means leaders making themselves dispensable and making groups so autonomous and strong that they don't need external direction. This leadership depends on trust, and trust is dependent on the personal and political integrity of leaders. It can only be maintained through openness in decision-making and it is only possible where people are consulted so that they continue to feel involved in the process. When a group is seen to want 'control' it is not trusted. This is why Militant failed to gain the trust of the movement despite the hard work of many of its activists.

Open leadership and support was not provided by the All-Britain Federation, but wherever it was needed, a multitude of new organisations emerged to fill the gaps. Soon a host of national newsletters were available. These included *3D* and *Refuse and Resist*. Workshops and day schools were organised to bring together activists from across Britain on a regular basis. These were far more practical than national federation set-piece conferences which only discussed motions and amendments to motions, once a year. Other organisations such as the Poll Tax Legal Group emerged to provide technical specialist support. The TSDC filled the gap which was left after the inflammatory statements made by Tommy Sheridan and Steve Nally about Trafalgar Square demonstrators.

Because of the grass roots nature of the Anti-Poll Tax movement it was able to support the emergence of different centres of national leadership, encouraging those with specific skills or expertise to organise autonomously. Local Anti-Poll Tax Unions were able to choose which national initiatives to support and from where they got the information and technical support that they needed. This prevented the core of the movement from stagnating, because people moved to where the strongest energy for action lay.

If there had only been one highly centralised focus of leadership, the campaign would have been more vulnerable to attack from the state and the media. It is easy for them to mount

Opposite: Hundreds of national and local newsletters were created to fulfil the information needs of the movement.

3D on't pay!
on't collect!
on't implement!

Issue #4 of the open, independant newsletter produced by the 3D network

go for it!

SOUTH LONDON   November 1990

Fight the Poll Tax!   Issue 1

MOBILISE N

Wandsworth Council, with Beresford at the hel—
long been condsidered the Tories flagship counci— ·
was at the head of the Tories initiative t—
provision, and long ago proved—
collusion of the local trad—
class resistance

REFUSE AND RESIST.

NEWS FROM LOCAL ANTI-POLL TAX GROUPS

FIRST QUARTER 1991

PRICE: BY DONATION

ISSUE No.6

"Smash The Tories"

"No Poll Tax Here"

"No War But The Class W

WAR
Poll Tax

Council Gets Red Ca

For the 3rd year running,
Council meeting on 28th
set the new Poll Tax w
by independent anti-poll ta

In a restricted gallery,
reluctantly agreed to
inst the poll tax.
Andy Clachirs
ge left with
from
nont c
politio
on-pa
to sto
es ag

STOCKBRIDGE NEW TOWN ANTI POLL TAX NEWS

ONE MILLION NON PAYERS IN SCO

t pay - the po
hands

smear campaigns against individuals who have been delegated authority (Arthur Scargill was the classic example of this) but it is virtually impossible to attack a localised mass movement with no leaders. In the Anti-Poll Tax movement no national individual or group had constitutional power, and most had limited influence. When the media attacked Steve Nally for stirring up riots, it made no difference, because most ordinary activists didn't even know who he was.

Yet, despite this, organisations such as Militant persisted in their belief in centralised forms of leadership. Even though over 17 million people had refused to pay the tax, and 200,000 had demonstrated in March 1990, the All-Britain Federation was prepared to negotiate with the TUC about calling a joint demonstration which jettisoned the banner of non-payment. This implied that they thought it was more important to win the support of the labour movement leaders, than to keep the support of those on low incomes who were already behind the non-payment campaign. Once again we see a failure to understand where political power lies. Indeed, if the labour movement had taken up the leadership, it is likely that the Anti-Poll Tax movement would have fallen apart. As Bob Goupillot from Prestonfield suggests:

> The important thing about the Anti-Poll Tax campaign, that made it different from all other campaigns, is that old thing of self activity. People stopped waiting around for the Labour Party and trade union leaders. They said, 'Well we don't really know what to do, but we'll have a go,' and they worked it out, and they got organised. The thing we must avoid at all costs is leading our struggle, which we have built, back into those channels which have been leading us up the garden path at least since 1945. As soon as people accept the leadership of those people they will wind the struggle down, back into safe constitutional channels, and that worries me. I remember

people shouting 'Neil Kinnock give us a
lead!' – that's illusion building not resistance building.

Bob Goupillot, 4th Scottish Anti Poll Tax Forum, 11/4/91.

When responsibility is handed over to leaders,
people expect them to do the work and relin-
quish the personal and collective responsibility
which gives them power. This is the sad history
of many potential revolutionary struggles in
Britain.

The Importance Of Community

The Anti-Poll Tax campaign was launched
from local communities because it was in these
communities that there was still mass involvement.

Over decades, capitalism has fragmented
society, breaking people up so they no longer
come together to organise. Home ownership
broke the tie of a shared landlord; weakening
work-place organisation prevented people
from sharing their work experience; breaking
up local shopping streets and creating shop-
ping-centres literally stopped people meeting
in the streets. Yet, while capitalism has been
extremely effective at breaking up communities of workers, it has also created a potential for
strengthening neighbourhood communities.
This is because those who are less well-off have
increasingly been locked into run-down inner-
city areas and sprawling suburban housing
estates. The Mayfield estate is a typical example:

Our area is mostly made up of housing
schemes. There isn't a big shopping area. It
was a mining community but then they
closed down the pit, so there's a high
unemployment rate in this area. The centre
of Mayfield is the Labour Club, everything

197

goes on in there. Its a built up area, there's
not a lot of play for the kids. There's a small
community centre, nothing else around
here. But we pay high bus fares if we go
into town.
Chris Moyers, Mayfield APTU, 6/5/91.

It was these conditions which provided the
basis for solidarity during the Anti-Poll Tax
campaign. On the Mayfield Estate, ten miles or
so from the centre of Edinburgh, bus fares were
too expensive for people to travel regularly out
of the area. People were isolated with little to
do. But this meant that when a high profile
campaign came along, everyone wanted to
participate.

People didn't have to make an effort to
become involved in these communities, they
were already involved. They went to the local
shops and talked to each other every day; they
used their community centres; they talked to
their neighbours across the garden fence; parents met each other outside the school gates, in
the nurseries and playgrounds – they organised collective child-care for their children;
people met and talked at the local laundry and
did their washing together – they went to the
local pub or the football match together. Networks of families and friends; lollypop men
and women; local mini-cab drivers; milkmen
and postwomen interacted daily. Sometimes
these community links became visible forms of
public life – like tenants' associations – agitat-
ing against injustice. Sometimes they remained
hidden to the outside world, but they were
always there.

The Anti-Poll Tax Unions were able to tap
into these networks because they were run by
ordinary local people who were trusted. Because they were locally based, it was possible to
organise practical resistance. This relied on
quick communication, a good knowledge of
the local area, and people who were close at
hand to provide direct support. Likewise, to
keep the community confident, people had to
know that their neighbours were still not paying, and that they were not on their own. This

was information which could only be transferred through informal local networks. Local people understood this, and as the Anti-Poll Tax campaign grew so the links between different parts of the community developed:

> See in this area, there's still gang warfare which goes on between all the local communities. But now the likes of myself, I can go into the youth centre in the area and they recognise me because of the Poll Tax struggle, and they'll speak to me. Before, a guy walking down the road and there was ten or twelve of them standing there, they would jump on the guy and give him a doing, give him a hammering. Whereas I can walk in there and speak to them and they'll speak to us cos they know that we're fighting not just for ourselves, we're fighting for the next generation.
>
> *Jackie Moyers, Mayfield APTU, 6/5/91.*

On estates like Mayfield, there was little for kids to do other than hang around. But the Anti-Poll Tax struggle gave them something, other than each other, to fight. Similar changes came about on the Prestonfield estate in Edinburgh:

> We have a method of putting out boards. At the top of the avenue; at the end of the streets; at the bus stop – focal points. It's amazing most of these notices remain, the kids in this estate didn't bother about the boards. I could put them out, go to work and come back and they would still be there.
>
> *Sadie Rooney, Prestonfield Community Resistance 10/5/91.*

This demonstrated an awareness and respect for the Anti-Poll Tax campaign. People of all ages realised that they should be fighting on the same side against a common enemy. So, not only did the community provide the base for the struggle, but the struggle strengthened the community.

There are many examples of the way in which this happened. Women based at home

became the backbone of the campaign, often taking on most of the organisational and political tasks. For some this was the first time that their work in the community had been explicitly valued. Many women (as in the miners' strike) were profoundly changed by the campaign:

> Myself, I don't know what will happen after the Poll Tax. I just cannot see me returning to being just an ordinary housewife. I want to go to college in September, and I hope to take politics and sociology.
> *Chris Moyers, Mayfield APTU, 6/5/91.*

Other changes took place in the neighbourhoods:

> The barriers of age, sex, and race began to crumble. Ali, the local Asian shopkeeper allowed us to stick a huge notice-board in his shop window. The local launderette took leaflets. Some people became noticeably healthier. Mary McInnes, one of the oldest members of the Prestonfield group, who occasionally needed a ventilator to breathe, and at first needed a lift to meetings, literally ran up the street to be at Paul Smart's house before the sheriff officers.
> *Bob Goupillot, Prestonfield Community Resistance, 13/8/91.*

But it was not only people who changed, there was also a change in perception. Before the Anti-Poll Tax campaign, debt was something people were ashamed of. Proud working class families paid their debts and if necessary went without food in order to do so. After it, many realised that the bills they were being asked to pay were not reasonable or legitimate. And people began to apply the same criteria to other bills as they had to the Poll Tax:

> You've got prescription charges, you've got rising rents, you've got bus fares continually rising; you've got low wages – there's a lot of poverty. I only bring home about £93 a week. If you take the Poll Tax and the rent

Opposite:

the Somerset Clarion –

journal of the Somerset

Community Defence

Campaign – is one of the

most respected socialist

publications in the South

West. It is known for its

rejection of sectarianism,

and regularly carries

articles from groups as

diverse as the Labour Party,

the Green Party, Militant,

the SWP, Class War etc, as

well as many non – aligned

individuals.

201

and electricity off £93 you're not left with much. In fact if the rents continue to rise, then I'll not be paying the rent. It's as simple as that. I mean, you can't get blood out of a stone

Sadie Rooney, Prestonfield Community Resistance, 10/5/91.

As a result of this change in perception, some groups started to extend the struggle to include all debts. In Edinburgh for example, local Anti-Poll Tax groups mobilised against an eviction for rent arrears on April 9th 1991. This may be an important avenue for future action. There is no reason why there should be any difference between a sheriff officers action for non-payment of the Poll Tax, and one for non-payment of rent, electricity or anything else.

Because the informal networks of the community have not been as weakened as the labour and trade union movements, they will remain, for some time, the strongest base for political action. This will require new forms of community based resistance, which focus on more than on a single issue. There are already examples of successful community resistance campaigns. A few, like the Somerset Community Defence Campaign have been operating since the miners strike. Such organisations are likely to be important vehicles for radical change in the future, becoming part of a new politics of the Left.

Society will not be fundamentally changed by attempts to influence the parliamentary process (as exemplified by the Labour Party), or by setting up small groupings to be the vanguard of a revolution (like Militant and the SWP). The organisations which take on the struggle will need to be decentralised and diverse, based upon participation not representation. They will need to be founded on a politics of mass-action which has the power not just to protest but to resist oppresion and create change. The Anti-Poll Tax movement may have been the start of that process, but there is a lot more to come.

Glossary

Bailiffs
See sheriff officers.

Capping
A power imposed by central government to limit the amount of spending (and therefore the level of local taxation) which a local authority could make.

Community Charge
The official term for the Poll Tax.

McKenzie friend
McKenzie friends were people who were allowed to stand beside a defendant in court and offer them advice although they were not allowed to address the court. Anti Poll Tax activists trained with legal knowledge acted as McKenzie friends as part of the strategy of delaying the court process.

Liability order
A liability order was a piece of paper given to the council after courts (in England and Wales) had proved that non-payers were liable to pay the tax. Once a liability order was granted councils were free to proceed with enforcement procedures (bailiff action or wage arrestment). This procedure was not necessary in Scotland.

Poinding
Poindings describe the process whereby sheriff officers enter peoples homes and value their goods.

Sheriff officer
The equivalent of bailiffs in England and Wales, people who were appointed by local councils and registered by local courts with powers to seize peoples possessions and sell them off to recover debts.

Warrant sale
These were public auctions of peoples goods (sometimes held in their own homes) after they had been seized by the Sheriff Officers. By November 1991, there hadn't been a single successful warrant sale in Scotland.

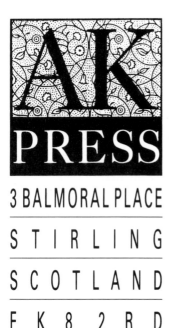

3 BALMORAL PLACE

S T I R L I N G

S C O T L A N D

F K 8 2 R D

FURTHER *AK PRESS* TITLES

terrorizing the neighbourhood
American Foreign Policy in the Post-Cold War Era
Noam Chomsky
Preface by **James Kelman**
ISBN 1 873176 00 7 £3.95

Traces the origins, goals and implications of US foreign policy in the years following World War II. Written in a rigourous but accessible style, this book serves as a short introduction and primer to this major thinker's work on US foreign affairs: its causes, effects, and the interests it serves, both at home and abroad.

the bigger tory vote
The Covert Sequestration of the Bigotry Vote
Nick Toczek
ISBN 1 873176 20 1 £2.95

Investigates the absorption of neo-fascist, racist and other far-right elements into the Conservative Party since the late 1940s.

the assault on culture
Utopian Currents from Lettrisme to Class War
Stewart Home
ISBN 1 873176 30 9 £5.95

"A concise introduction to a whole mess of troublemakers through the ages... well-written, incisive and colourful."
(N.M.E.)

leonard's shorter catechism
Tom Leonard
ISBN 1 873176 25 2 £1.95

A series of satirical questions and answers on the Gulf War and its aftermath by the celebrated Scots poet; with a preface in which he examines the role of the media in reporting the war.

For our latest mailorder catalogue, featuring these and several thousand other titles, please send a large SAE/IRCs to AK Distribution, 3 Balmoral Place, Stirling, Scotland, FK8 2RD.

We're a small group of people who have come together to produce propaganda because we're sick of trying to survive in a world where we're ripped off, bossed around and treated like objects. The solution to the problems that face us is not the Labour Party, the Green Party or the tiny left-wing parties, but *revolution*: overthrowing the existing social set-up and building a new world run not for profit, but to satisfy our needs.

We have produced the following publications:

ATTACK
INTERNATIONAL

BM 6577
LONDON
WC1N 3XX
ENGLAND

breaking free
ISBN 0 9514261 0 9   £2.00
The real adventures of Tintin in a classic full-length cartoon tale of love, struggle and revolution. "Naive and brutish" *(Sunday Times)*, "Absolutely terrible" *(Police Federation)*, "Hilarious" *(The Face)*.

the free
m. gilliland
ISBN 0 9514261 3 3   £3.00
A gripping novel of a revolutionary upheaval in modern-day Europe. Passionate, powerful and convincing.

the spirit of freedom
ISBN 0 9514261 1 7   £1.00
A short and punchy booklet about the war in Ireland which shows exactly why British troops were sent in again in 1969, and why it's in our interests to get them out.

until all are free
ISBN 0 9514261 2 5   £0.50
The trial statement of Ray Luc Levasseur, jailed for 45 years for conspiring to overthrow the United States government.

poll tax riot
NOT AN ATTACK PUBLICATION   £1.00
The inside story of the battle of Trafalgar Square: eight hours that rocked the nation.

Support Poll Tax Prisoners!

The state has tried to use jailings to crush resistance to the poll tax. Over 100 people were jailed after the poll tax demonstrations in Trafalgar Square and Brixton in 1990, and some remain in prison. Already by the end of 1991, 120 people had been jailed for non-payment and millions more are facing the threat of similar action. Others face imprisonment for resisting bailiffs.

Support for people facing the police, the courts and the prisons has been one of the most encouraging aspects of the anti-poll tax movement. There have been many pickets of prisons in this country, and there have also been protests in support of poll tax prisoners all around the world, including in Russia, Poland, France and Canada. Still it is important that this level of support is maintained, and indeed stepped up.This support is the responsibility of the poll tax movement as a whole. We have to show our rulers that we will not allow them to use hostages to intimidate non-payers and scare people away from demonstrating.

The Poll Tax Prisoners Support Network was set up to co-ordinate practical and political support for our prisoners. Everybody can help by:
● writing to prisoners to show them and the prison authorities that they have not been forgotten. An up to date prisoners list is available from the network.
● giving us details of any prisoners you know who want support.
● sending us money to help us in our work.
● fighting for an amnesty for all poll tax prisoners and non-payers.

Poll Tax Prisoners Support Network, c/o 506 Brixton Rd, London SW9. Telephone: 071 738 7586.

mark simmons is a photographer/photojournalist based in Bristol. The images appearing in this book are a small selection of a much larger archive covering most aspects of the anti-Poll Tax campaign.

If you are interested in holding an exhibition on the Poll Tax or commissioning other documentary work, please contact Mark at 24 St Werburghs Park, Bristol, BS2 9YS. Tel 0272 **351241**